Genghis Khan and the Mongols

Towards the end of the twelfth century, Mongol nomads descended in hordes from the barren steppes of Central Asia and spread confusion and terror among the civilized states of the West. Cities were razed to the ground, and men, women and children slaughtered like cattle.

The author traces the ruthless rise to power of the Mongol leader Genghis Khan, from his youth as a friendless refugee to his later years as Khan of all the Mongols, ruler of one of the world's largest empires. Yet, within a hundred years, this great empire had collapsed, leaving behind it little but legend – tales of great warriors, and savage punishments, of men who drank blood from their horses' necks, and buried their enemies alive beneath mounds of stones.

The book is lavishly illustrated with contemporary pictures, as well as specially commissioned diagrams and maps, which give a fascinating insight into the little-known world of the Mongols.

A WAYLAND SENTINEL BOOK

Genghis Khan and the Mongols

Michael Gibson

"The greatest joy for a man is to defeat his enemies, to drive them before him, to take from them all they possess, to see those they love in tears, to ride their horses, and to hold their wives and daughters in his arms." *Genghis Khan*

WAYLAND PUBLISHERS LONDON

More Sentinel Books

frontispiece   A Mongol trader supervises the loading of his camel.

SBN 85340 186 1

Copyright © 1973 by Wayland (Publishers) Ltd.
101 Grays Inn Road, London WC1
Set in 'Monophoto' Baskerville and printed offset litho by
Page Bros (Norwich) Ltd.

Contents

List of Illustrations

Introduction

"In this year of 1240, a detestable nation of Satan, and by this I mean the countless army of Tartars, broke loose from its mountain-guarded home. Piercing the solid rocks of the Caucasus, they poured forth like devils from the hell of Tartarus. They swarmed locust-like over the face of the earth, and brought terrible devastation to the eastern parts of Europe, laying it waste with fire and carnage."

This was how Matthew of Paris, a thirteenth-century monk, described a race of nomads called the Mongols. To the Christians, they were "the nation of Satan," to the Moslems, "the Accursed of God," to the Chinese, "the Godless ones."

They wandered with their herds over the bare steppes of Central Asia. For centuries, this area had been a breeding ground for fierce warriors, the Huns and the Turks, who attacked the rich and settled empires of the world. But how was it that a few thousand Asian nomads were able to cause panic in all the civilized states of the medieval world?

In Western Europe, the feudal kings and emperors were fully occupied in the attempt to win back the Holy Lands in Palestine from the Moslems, the followers of the prophet Mohammed. Crusade after crusade had been launched against the "infidel" without success. The rulers of medieval Europe were so absorbed in this that they didn't realize for a long time that the Mongols too posed a threat, not only to their way of life, but to their very existence.

The eastern boundaries of Europe had for many centuries been defended by the Christians of the Byzantine Empire, with its capital at Constantinople. This ancient empire, however, had been attacked and fatally weakened by the knights of the Fourth Crusade (1202–4). This meant that the Mediterranean world was now wide open to attack from the east.

A tribe of reindeer nomads in northern Mongolia. While the tribe is on the move, babies and young children are carried in cradles slung from the reindeer.

8

To the north of Constantinople lay the weak states of Bulgaria, Hungary and Poland, and beyond them the vast expanse of Russia. Here the Vikings had established trade routes, and built flourishing cities like Vladimir and Kiev. However, their great days were past. Jealousy and conflicting ambitions had destroyed their unity. There was little to stop a determined invader from conquering Eastern Europe.

9

Troubled lands

The Moslem Middle East was no better prepared to face the Mongols than Europe. The Turks had conquered Asia-Minor, Syria, Palestine and Egypt before collapsing, and these areas were now the scene of constant warfare.

Between the Tigris and the Euphrates lay the lands of the once mighty Caliph of Baghdad, "the Commander of the Faithful." Although he was still the religious head of the Moslem world, by far the most powerful Moslem ruler was now Aludin Muhammad, Shah of Khwarizm. The Shah ruled Persia, Turkestan and Afghanistan, and had earned the title of "the Victorious" on many fields of battle. But even he was no longer as strong as he had been — his people were divided over questions of religion, and deeply resented the heavy taxes the Shah demanded.

To the east of Khwarizm lay the empires of the Kara-Khitai and the Hsi-Hsia. Both these states were weak and unstable, their rulers kept in power by the armed forces. Nevertheless, they were important centres of learning. Their walled towns contained fine Buddhist temples and libraries, beautiful Christian churches and Moslem mosques.

Beyond them lay the vast lands of China, ruled by the Kin in the north and the Sung in the south. The Kin were protected by the Great Wall of China, along which six men could ride abreast. Their rich lands teemed with people. In the south, the Sung ruled a land whose tiny upper class enjoyed a world endowed with the finest porcelain, the most beautiful paintings and the loveliest fabrics, achieved through the harsh toil of countless poverty-stricken peasants. Both these Chinese states were in decline and looked fearfully towards the steppes, expecting at any minute that a new and terrible force of nomads

Below The Great Wall of China, built by the Chinese to protect their rich and prosperous kingdom.

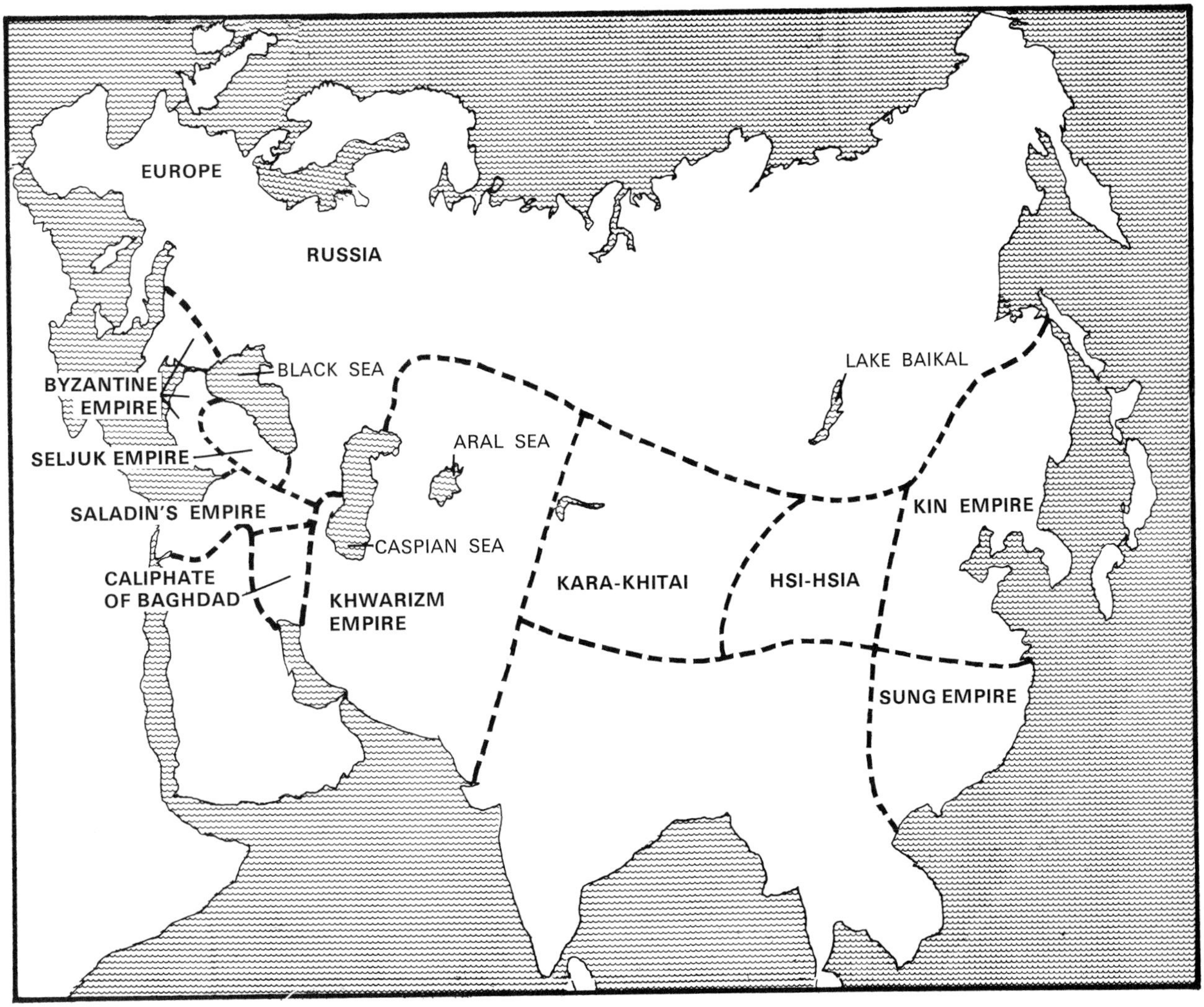
EUROPE
RUSSIA
BLACK SEA
BYZANTINE EMPIRE
SELJUK EMPIRE
SALADIN'S EMPIRE
CALIPHATE OF BAGHDAD
ARAL SEA
CASPIAN SEA
KHWARIZM EMPIRE
KARA-KHITAI
LAKE BAIKAL
HSI-HSIA
KIN EMPIRE
SUNG EMPIRE

Above Asia at the time of Genghis's birth.

would appear and bring fire and sword to their rich, settled lands.

And then, in 1206, the Mongols produced one of the greatest conquerors the world has ever known – Genghis Khan. He was not the first of his race to obtain great power. His great-grandfather, Kabul Khan, had united the Mongol tribes in the twelfth century, and had threatened to create a great empire. But he had been defeated and murdered by the Chinese, and the Mongols after him had sunk into obscurity.

1. Mongolia and the Mongols

In prehistoric times, Central Asia was a vast inland sea whose waters slowly evaporated, leaving behind two huge salt lakes, the Caspian and Aral seas. Where once waves lapped, lush grasses now grow. These prairies form a gigantic plateau about 4,000 feet above sea-level, which divides into three terraces: the plain of Outer Mongolia, the Gobi desert, and the grasslands of Inner Mongolia.

This immense area is bounded by mighty, snow-capped mountain ranges: the Urals, the Hindu Kush, the Himalayas, the Tien Shan and the Altai. To the south lie the sandy, waterless deserts of the Gobi, burning hot in summer and freezing cold in winter. To the north, great forests stretch right up to the Siberian tundra. Deep rivers water the plains: the Yenisei, the Ob, the Irtysh, the Tobol, the Ili, the Syr Darya and the Amu Darya.

The climate is harsh. In winter, furious blizzards sweep over the steppes, covering them with a deep blanket of snow, and turning the great rivers into solid beds of ice. The spring thaw brings new life. Plants germinate and grow, turning the grasslands into a carpet of flowers. In summer, these flowers wither and die; the green grass becomes dry, brown hay beneath the burning sun. The heat is unbearable. Next, towering banks of black cloud announce a season of violent and terrifying storms. After the thunder and lightning have passed, there comes the cool, dry air of the Indian summer, the best time of the year. During autumn, the cold gradually intensifies, and bitter winds sweep the land, followed by dark snow laden clouds. Winter rules once more.

On the steppes, the Mongol people spent most of their lives wandering from one grazing ground to another with their herds. They moved north and south with the seasons, following age-old routes.

Opposite The mountains and rivers of Mongolia.

Below Camel train crossing the Gobi desert, the harsh homeland of the Mongols.

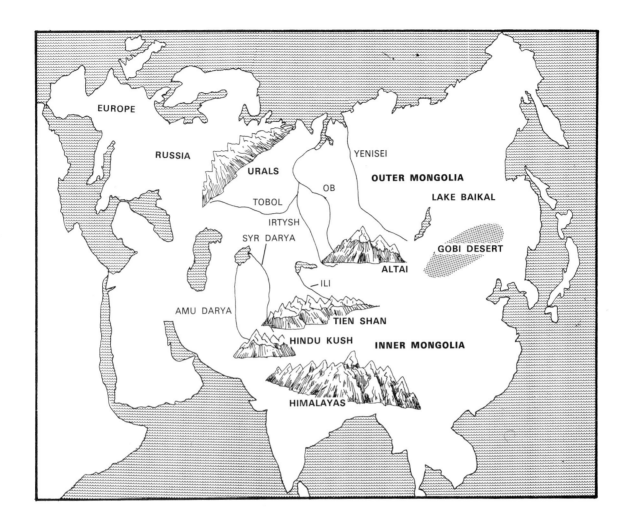

However, along the river valleys, there were also farmers who tilled the soil and lived a settled life. The nomads and the farmers existed side by side, but they were ill at ease with each other. In good times, there was a grudging understanding, and the two communities traded peacefully. But bad times sent the wild horsemen of the steppes down into the farmlands to take by the sword what they could not afford to pay for.

This was the world of the Asian nomad.

The Mongols

The Mongols were broad but short men, rarely more than five feet six inches tall. Their short, bandy legs seemed to have been specially designed to fit round a horse. Dark slanted eyes stared out from flat, yellow faces, marked by high cheekbones and small noses with flaring nostrils. They had little or no beard on their chins, but their heads were covered with coarse, black hair. They shaved the top of their

The Mongols were great horsemen. Their short, bandy legs seemed made to fit round a horse.

heads, and twisted the rest of their hair into long, greasy plaits.

"Their women," wrote one visitor, "are wondrously fat. The less nose they have, the more beautiful they are considered. They disfigure themselves hideously by painting their faces." The women's hairstyles reflected their position in society: young, unmarried girls wore their hair long, married women cut their hair back from their foreheads, and widows shaved off all their hair.

Both men and women wore similar clothes: long, leather fur-lined coats called "del," which were open from top to bottom and folded over the chest, with tight leather trousers and thick tall boots. Simple fur caps completed the men's outfit, while the women decked themselves out with great round hats, which were made on wooden frames and covered with costly materials. During the bitterly cold winters, they wore two sets of clothing, one set with the fur turned inside and the other with it out.

The Mongol nation consisted of a number of tribes. Each tribe was divided into clans, whose members were all descended from the same ancestor. There could be as few as a dozen or as many as several hundred households in any one clan. For most of the year, these families were scattered all over their grazing lands, and only came together in the summer when the pastures were rich and game was plentiful. Then they would pitch their tents in a great circle called a "Kuriyen," and make merry. This was the time to celebrate weddings, enjoy feasts and hold councils.

The rulers of these tribes were known as Khans. Their power depended on the strength of their personalities and also on their success in war. At the time of Genghis's birth, the Mongols were without a Great Khan, and tribe fought with tribe and clan against clan.

Below Typical Mongolian features: slanted, slit eyes, flat face, small nose and high cheekbones.

Marriage and the family

Because they were all so closely related, members of the same clan were forbidden to marry. It was therefore very difficult for the young men to find wives. Sometimes they would ride off to a neighbouring camp, and carry away some of the women, but this caused bloody wars. A much safer and more usual way was for the parents to arrange marriages for their children while these were still infants. The children would then be betrothed, and married as soon as they came of age.

The marriage was sealed by an exchange of gifts. The husband-to-be had to give his father-in-law a "brideprice" to compensate him for the loss of his daughter's services. Often a considerable amount of property was involved, and most of this brideprice would be provided by the groom's father, who would also give his son tents, horses, flocks and a share of his grazing grounds. In return, the girl's father gave his daughter a dowry, which she took with her to her husband's tent.

Weddings were riotous affairs, with much feasting and drinking. When the guests had finished eating, musicians would begin to play a tune softly and slowly. This would draw the men to their feet. At first, they swaggered around the camp fires, showing off their fine clothes. Gradually, however, the music and the dancing quickened till they were whirling and leaping high in the air. These barbaric ballets continued throughout the night until sheer exhaustion ended them at daybreak.

A man could have any number of wives, provided he could pay for them. The women accepted this custom quite readily, since there was too much work for any one woman to do in a Mongol household. A man's first wife was usually his chief wife, and was treated with respect by her younger rivals.

Above Inside a yurt. Note that, apart from the chests, there is very little furniture.

Opposite A Mongolian musician. See how even his instrument is decorated with a horse's head.

Each wife had her own tent and belongings, and lived apart from the others. However, they all helped with the daily chores.

If a man died while his children were still young, his chief widow became head of the family until her sons grew up and got married. If, on the other hand, a man died after most of his sons had already married, his wives, his tents and all his property went to his youngest son.

In spite of many tensions, the Mongol family was very close-knit.

Work and homelife

Among Mongols, there was a clear division between men's and women's work. The men undertook dangerous tasks that involved short bursts of concentrated effort, like the defence of the camp or hunting for food, while the women did relatively safe work, which entailed more prolonged but less strenuous exertion.

According to a Western traveller, William of Rubruck, "the men make bows and arrows, manufacture stirrups and bits, and make saddles. They build the tents and carts, take care of the horses and milk the mares. They churn the koumiss and make the skins in which it is kept. They also look after the camels and load them." Much of their time was spent hunting. Wild animals were tracked, driven into carefully prepared traps and slaughtered. Trained falcons brought down the winged game they could not reach with their bows and arrows. The Mongols used to say; "A man's greatest joy is to go out hunting on a fine, swift horse with a falcon on his wrist when the grass turns green."

Mongol women were proud, and much freer than their European contemporaries. They were the mistresses of their tents and of the family property. They traded with travelling merchants, and took charge when their husbands were away hunting or fighting. Riding astride like their menfolk, they could bring down a wolf with a single arrow as skilfully as any man.

"The women employ themselves," wrote William, "guiding the wagons, loading pack animals, making butter and dressing skins. They also make sandals, socks and other garments, and felt for the tents." This felt was made by beating and oiling animal hair until it formed a thick fabric.

Their beehive tents or yurts consisted of a framework of wooden poles covered by layers of felt, with a hole in the roof to let the light in and the smoke out. Apart from a few beautifully lacquered chests, some skins and rugs, iron pots and leather bags, there was little furniture, since everything had to be able to be packed into a small ox-drawn cart to be carried from place to place.

The tents were always pitched facing south. The women slept on the east side of the tent and the men on the west. The men never trespassed into the women's area, as this brought bad luck. Both men and women were watched over by household gods, represented by felt dolls called "the master's brother" and the "mistress's brother."

Hunting wild boar was a favourite sport for Mongol men. It provided them with food, and was also good training in horsemanship.

Food and cooking

The Mongols ate the flesh of dormice, marmots, wild sheep, gazelles, rabbits and even dogs. A Christian traveller was shocked to find a man eating the lice off his son's back, but the nomad only laughed and said: "Why shouldn't I eat them, haven't they been eating my son's flesh and drinking his blood?" Nor did they hesitate to eat the carcasses of any dead animals they found.

However, their staple foods were curds, butter, cheese and koumiss. To make koumiss, "the men pour mare's milk into a large skin and churn it with a special stick which is as big as a man's head and is hollowed out at its lower end. When they beat it quickly, the milk bubbles like new wine, turns sour and ferments. They churn it until they can extract the butter. Then, when it is fairly pungent, they drink it." Koumiss was unique since it was both a food and an alcoholic drink.

The women made butter out of cow's milk, and then boiled the remaining buttermilk until it curdled. The curds were dried in the sun and stored until wintertime, when they were mixed with hot water and drunk as a substitute for fresh milk.

Although much of the food they ate was uncooked, every Mongol family kept a stewpot full of leftovers from previous meals. As soon as they made camp at night, this pot was put to simmer on an open fire of thornbush or dung. According to William of Rubruck, the Mongols made superb horsemeat sausages, which were much better than European pork sausages, and were eaten raw. He also saw them making "charqui" by "cutting meat into thin strips and hanging it in the sun, so that it dries without salt and without any unpleasant smell." Sometimes they would put raw meat under their saddles or between their clothes, to press out all the

blood before drying and smoking it.

Their eating habits were disgusting, even by medieval standards. They hacked at their meat with hunting knives, tore off great lumps and stuffed them into their mouths. Knowing what it was to starve, in times of plenty they would eat until they choked. Instead of washing their plates and spoons, they would dip them into the game pot and rinse them in the stew. Then they would wipe their greasy fingers on their clothes or in the grass.

Men making koumiss from mare's milk.

21

Crime and punishment

Before Genghis Khan came to power, Mongol society was in a bad way. Rape and murder were everyday occurrences. Whenever a member of one clan was hurt by a member from another, a blood feud resulted. The Mongols believed in taking "an eye for an eye and a tooth for a tooth." However, the

Mongol punishments were often harsh and brutal.

incident was not closed when the injured party had been avenged, because the kinsmen of the punished man would in turn demand vengeance. And so the feud would carry on for generation after generation, poisoning the life of the community.

But the Mongols were not uncivilized barbarians. They believed in the rule of law, and enforced it whenever possible. Property was fiercely protected. The Mongols did not lock up their valuables, and theft was easy. To combat this, thieves and the receivers of stolen property were savagely punished. Western visitors to the Mongol empire were most impressed by the honesty of the people, and the absence of robbers. If animals wandered away from their herds, they were nearly always returned to their rightful owners by those who found them.

Until Genghis's reign, capital punishment had been rare except in cases where the culprit was actually caught committing a crime. Most crimes were punished by beatings; the guilty party would receive between seven and 107 lashes, depending on the gravity of his offence. Adultery and highway robbery were punished by death, as was sorcery.

When Genghis came to power, he drew up a code of laws called the Yasa, which created many new offences and prescribed severe penalties. The Mongols were not allowed to urinate in the rivers, nor to wash in them. Their clothes were not to be washed, but had to be worn until they fell to pieces. No man was to be persecuted for his religion. Any man disobeying a royal order was to be executed. Anyone who took part in a blood feud was to be put to death.

When a man was accused of wrongdoing, he either admitted his guilt or else swore that he was innocent. If it was later discovered that he had lied, he was executed for breaking his word.

During his lifetime, Genghis reduced crime amongst Mongols to a minimum, and encouraged them to be honest, law-abiding and loyal.

23

Religion and the shamans

The Mongols were a religious people. They believed that the world was full of invisible forces of evil, which came out of the Kanum Kotan, the north Siberian plain. These wicked demons were controlled by the spirit of the "Everlasting Blue Sky." To keep on the right side of this mighty spirit, they sacrificed men and white horses on the top of high hills. Many lesser spirits were also thought to live in fire, running water and the wind. These too were treated with respect. Guardian spirits were said to watch over the reindeer, the gazelle and the great bears of the forest. Each clan also had its own animal spirit or totem; the Blue Wolf was the legendary ancestor of Genghis Khan and his family.

The Mongols venerated their ancestors, and believed that they watched over them. Each clan consisted of the dead, the living and those yet to be born. Mongol children learned the names of their ancestors as a sacred duty. They would model themselves upon them, and try to equal their legendary feats of valour. A man's first duty was to raise a family so that his ancestors would live on.

The only human beings who could contact these spirits were the mysterious shamans, who acted as priests, doctors, sorcerers and fortune-tellers. They held séances in the eerie stillness of the night. By the flickering campfires, they muttered their spells and incantations, and danced to the beat of a drum. Gradually, they would dance faster and faster until they had worked themselves into a frenzy and had to be overpowered and tied down. In a state of trance, they spoke with the spirits and answered the questions of their audience in unearthly voices.

The shamans were expert showmen, and created an awe-inspiring atmosphere, shrieking, groaning

The Mongols were very superstitious people, and held their shamans in great respect. In this picture, the woman is dancing to the beat of a drum. Soon she will fall into a trance, and speak with the spirits of the night.

and foaming at the mouth. Many of them were ventriloquists, who made it seem as if voices were coming from the empty air. Some may well have been hypnotists who could conjure up vivid pictures in the minds of their audience. Even though they had learned their tricks during a long and arduous apprenticeship, most of them sincerely believed in their powers.

During eclipses of the sun or moon, which terrified the Mongols, only the shamans dared to stay out in the open, beating their drums and casting their spells. They were feared and respected by everybody.

25

Witchcraft and oracles

The Mongols believed that every single thing that happened in life was planned; nothing happened by chance. If someone dropped a pot, or tripped and fell, then it was the work of a mischievous demon or sorcerer. They believed in "black" and "white" magic. Witches employed black magic to injure and even kill people, while good shamans used white

Opposite and below The
Mongol Khans seldom
made any decisions without
first consulting their
magicians and holy men,
who would advise them on
what to do.

magic to protect people from devils and witches.

They also believed that their enemies could be bewitched. Some Mongols certainly approached the shamans with this in mind. Today, most people don't believe in witchcraft, but in those days everybody did. It was a question of simple faith. Many Mongols were perfectly well aware that the shamans they saw were cheats, but they remained convinced that somewhere there were genuine ones. This faith helped to make the misfortunes of their life understandable and more bearable.

When the Mongols had difficult decisions to make, instead of weighing up the arguments for or against a particular solution, they would consult oracles. Sheep's shoulder blades were roasted until they cracked. If the cracks ran lengthwise, it was a sign that the plan was a good one and would succeed; but if they cracked horizontally, the plan was doomed to failure. The fate of whole nations was decided in this way. Many of the Great Khans never made up their minds about any course of action until they had consulted the oracles.

The study of the stars was another way of finding out about the future. As soon as a child was born, a shaman would cast his horoscope and predict how his life would unfold. When Mangu Khan's wife gave birth to a baby boy, the shamans prophesied that he would enjoy a long life and become a great ruler. A few days later, however, the baby died, and the shamans were summoned to appear before the angry Empress. They were ready with an explanation. The child, they said, had been murdered by the spirit of a witch who had been executed only a few days before his birth. In revenge, the Empress had the witch's son and daughter put to death. All the openings to their bodies were sewn up, then they were wrapped up in blankets and drowned in the nearby river. This was done so that their wicked spirits would be bottled up inside their dead bodies for ever.

Sickness and death

The Mongols believed that their illnesses were caused by wicked demons or witches. When the Emperor Ogedai became ill, the shamans were of the opinion that demons had taken possession of his body, so they sealed his tent and beat their drums outside his door for some time. Then they swept out his yurt with birch brooms, and heated a mixture of pure spring water, milk and wine. When they bathed the Khan's body with this liquid, he recovered, and their reputations were made.

On another occasion, when an important woman was taken sick, the shamans ordered her maid to feel the painful part of her mistress's body. To her astonishment, the girl discovered what she thought was a piece of felt. But when she put it on the ground, "it began to crawl like a live thing." The shamans told the woman that she had been bewitched. She too recovered.

When a chief was taken ill, he would shut himself up in his tent and display a black tufted staff outside his door to warn the passers-by. The only people allowed to come near him were the shamans. If he died, his relatives mourned him with loud wails. But their grief was eased by the knowledge that they would not have to pay any taxes for the rest of the year.

The corpse was dressed in his finest clothes and jewellery, and placed in a deep grave with a supply of food and drink. Usually a mare, a stallion and a foal were also placed in the tomb, so that the chief could raise a herd of horses in the next world. Sometimes, his wives were strangled and buried with him. In some graves, archaeologists have found the remains of yurts and wagons. The tomb was carefully covered with earth and grass to hide it from the greedy eyes of grave robbers. Anybody unfortunate

enough to meet a funeral procession was put to death. Marco Polo, the great medieval explorer who visited Mongolia in the thirteenth century, claimed that 20,000 people were executed on one occasion because the mourners had forgotten to warn the local people of their approach.

Once the burial was over, the mourners had to be purified. Two huge fires were lit side by side, and all the dead man's animals and relations filed between them and were sprinkled with holy water. Then life returned to normal.

A staff with a black horsehair tuft placed outside a yurt showed that the man inside was ill. It was a warning to everyone but the shamans to keep away.

Left Timujin and his mother pursuing the troops who had deserted them on Yesugei's death – an imaginary episode depicted in a fifteenth-century Persian manuscript.

Below One of the few surviving portraits of Genghis Khan.

2. Genghis Khan

By the side of the River Onon, in 1167, a Mongol woman called Hoelun gave birth to a boy named Timujin. He was to grow up to become Genghis Khan, "the World Conqueror." His great grandfather had been the mighty Kabul Khan, whose empire was destroyed by the Kin Chinese in the twelfth century. His father, Yesugei-Bagatur (the

30

Brave), commanded a small warband or "ulus," like many other Mongol leaders. He had captured his wife, the beautiful Hoelun, during an attack on a Merkit camp where she was waiting to be married. The Merkit never forgave him or his clan.

Timujin was the eldest of Yesugei's four sons by Hoelun. As the boy was growing up, Yesugei started to look about for a suitable wife for his eldest son. His choice fell upon Bortei, the daughter of Dai-Sechen, the chief of the powerful Konkurat tribe. Timujin was only eight and his wife-to-be nine when they were betrothed. Yesugei left his son at Dai-Sechen's camp to be educated as a guarantee of his good faith.

Later, Yesugei fell in with a band of Tartars while on a journey and, although they were traditional enemies, accepted an invitation to dine with them. Then, on his way home, he was taken violently ill, and realized that he had been poisoned. He dragged himself to his camp and sent off his servant, Munlik, to fetch his eldest son. Timujin rode night and day, but his father was dead by the time he reached the camp. At the age of nine, he had become head of the family. A hard road lay ahead of him.

All Yesugei's ulus, and even the faithful Munlik, deserted the fatherless family. Hoelun commented bitterly: "Except for our shadows, we have no friends." They lived by scavenging. Nevertheless, Hoelun never let her sons forget their great ancestors, whose "voices rolled like thunder in the mountains, whose hands were as strong as bears' paws and broke men in two as easily as arrows."

Although he was not as strong as his brothers Kasar and Bekter, Timujin grew up to be tall and proud. As the eldest son, he liked to have his own way. When he and his brother Bekter quarrelled, they fought literally to the death. Hoelun raged, "You are like mad dogs that rend their own flesh," but Timujin refused to be upset.

31

Hard times

Shortly after this, a neighbouring tribe, the Taichuts, raided Timujin's camp. Timujin fled into the forest and hid there until starvation drove him out. The Taichuts were waiting for him. They fixed a heavy wooden yoke around his neck and dragged him off. But, that evening, while his enemies celebrated their victory, Timujin knocked out his guard and made off into the night. When he reached the river Onon, he waded out into the current until only his head was above water. A friendly nomad found him and hid him in his yurt, while the Taichuts scoured the country for him. Next day, he smuggled him out of the camp in a wagonload of fleeces. As soon as it was safe, the nomad gave him a horse and sent him on his way.

Timujin followed the secret paths of the forest until he found his family on the slopes of Mount Burkhan-Kaldun. There they stayed for the next few years, hunting marmots and wild mice. Gradually, Timujin's confidence returned, and he claimed Bortei as his wife. Dai-Sechen honoured his promise to this penniless young man, and gave Bortei a black sable coat as her dowry.

Timujin now needed a powerful patron to further his career. So he went to the camp of Tugral, the chief of the Keraits, who had been his father's blood-brother, and gave him the sable coat as a gift. Tugral was pleased, and promised to help Timujin.

However, a band of Merkit then attacked Timujin's camp. Timujin only had time to seize his weapons before escaping, and he left his young wife to the tender mercies of the raiders. They carried her off and gave her to one of their warriors by whom she had a son, called Juchi. As soon as he heard of this disaster, Tugral sent Timujin reinforcements. The

Although captured and heavily yoked (*right*) by his enemies, Genghis managed to escape and conceal himself in the river (*opposite*).

young husband tracked the raiders to their camp and slaughtered every one of them. When Bortei was found unharmed in the chief's tent, Timujin called off the campaign.

For a year and half after that, Timujin and his followers rode with his blood-brother, Jamuga, who was the chief of the Juriats. However, Timujin soon realized that he could not become a great leader while he lived in the shadow of another man, so he and Jamuga parted. Later, their friendship turned to hatred, and they became bitter enemies.

The road to power

Many Mongols joined this strange, determined young man because he seemed destined to do great things. He established his reputation by a brilliant victory over his old enemies, the Taichuts. Throwing aside the traditional tactics of his people, he smashed his opponents with massed cavalry charges. He celebrated this victory by boiling the Taichut chiefs to death.

The Mongols elected him Khan and swore: "Now you are Khan, we shall fight in the forefront of every battle against your foes. When we capture beautiful girls, we shall give them to you. We shall leave for the chase at the crack of dawn and give all that we catch to you. If in battle we disobey your commands, or in peacetime injure your interests, you shall take our wives and possessions and leave us to our fate in the wilderness."

At first, the old chief Tugral was pleased by his adopted son's success. When the Kin Chinese wanted mercenaries for a war against the Tartars, the two of them fought side by side, earning the praise of all by their skill and courage. However, Tugral soon came to resent Timujin's rising power, and began to look for an opportunity to get rid of him.

Genghis showed his brilliance as a military leader by overwhelming his old enemies, the Taichuts.

His chance came during a campaign against a tribe called the Naiman. One night, the Keraits stole away and left the Mongols alone to face much superior forces. Timujin only managed to escape by making a rapid and undignified retreat.

Even after this treachery, Timujin continued to serve Tugral until Tugral's tribe, the Keraits, made a cowardly attack against him. Then Timujin had no choice but to destroy his false friend. He pretended to withdraw from Tugral's lands, and tricked the old man into believing that he was safe from attack. Then he swept down on the Kerait camp like a hawk. The Keraits fought well, but they had been caught by surprise and were overwhelmed. Tugral escaped but was soon hunted down and killed.

As a result, Timujin was master of central and eastern Mongolia. The young Khan had a strong sense of mission. He believed that he had been chosen by destiny to re-establish the power of the Mongols, and avenge the defeat of his great-grandfather, Kabul Khan. But, before he could do this, he had to conquer the remaining nomad tribes, and make himself undisputed ruler of them all.

35

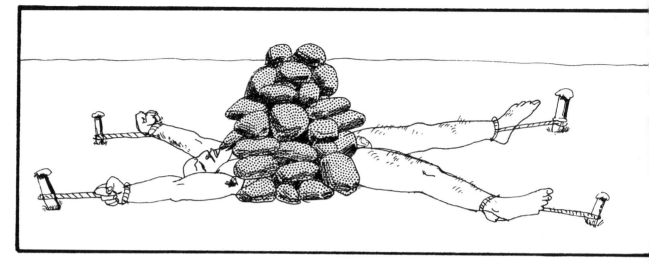

The year of the Leopard

Almost at once, Timujin received the opportunity he needed. Tayan Khan, chief of the Naiman, was also worried by Timujin's rise to power. He wrote to the chief of the Onguts: "We learn that in our neighbourhood a man has appeared styling himself 'Khan of the Mongols' and with his eyes fixed on the heavens. Just as a man cannot put two swords into the same scabbard, so there cannot be two rulers in the same realm. I beg you to become my right hand and help me to take away his bow and arrows." But Tayan Khan had misjudged his man. The Ongut chief immediately warned Timujin of his danger.

The following spring, Timujin marched against his enemies. According to the Naiman, the Mongols were like "hounds fed on human flesh, with skulls of brass, teeth of rock, tongues like needles and hearts of iron. Instead of horsewhips, they carry swords. They drink dew. They ride like the wind. In battle, they devour human flesh." In the ensuing battle, the Naiman were crushed, and all their generals killed. However, instead of taking his

Left The cruel death of Jamuga, Genghis's blood-brother.

Below 1206, the year of the Leopard. Timujin is elected Genghis Khan, the Khan of Khans, at a great meeting of the Mongol chiefs.

customary revenge, Timujin ordered the Naiman to be treated with respect. There was no looting or killing. Timujin married the dead chief's widow, and everything possible was done to reconcile the Naiman and bring about a union of the two peoples.

He spent the next year strengthening his hold over the country he had conquered. Of his enemies, only his blood-brother Jamuga remained. But Jamuga had fallen on evil days, and was reduced to leading a band of robbers. Fearing for their miserable lives, these men bound up their leader and delivered him to Timujin. Too much had passed between them for Timujin to show much mercy to his blood-brother. He ordered his men to kill Jamuga in such a way that not a drop of his blood would be shed. This was to prevent his blood-brother's spirit escaping from his body and haunting him. Jamuga was crushed to death by having rocks piled on his chest.

In the year of the Leopard, 1206, all the Mongol chieftains attended a great "Kuriltai" or conference on the banks of the river Onon. There Timujin was elected "Genghis Khan" or "Khan of Khans." Soon, he set about creating an army with which to conquer the world.

3. Army organization

Genghis Khan introduced the principle of universal service by which every adult Mongol, male or female, was expected to serve the Emperor. In war-time, the men fought in the army while the women performed all their duties back home. During peacetime, the men had to maintain the roads, and help in ruling the empire.

The army was divided into units: tens, hundreds, thousands and ten thousands or "tumans." The smaller units, the tens and hundreds, consisted of a single clan or group of clans, while the thousands were made up of clans from several different tribes. This was part of Genghis's plan to replace the old clan and tribal loyalties by allegiance to a single state.

Genghis Khan was a good judge of character, and he himself appointed all the ninety-five "noyans" who commanded the thousands. His generals like Jebei, Subodai and Mukali were great soldiers in their own right. He bound these men to him by his dynamic personality and generosity. The quality of his officer corps was maintained because he insisted that promotion should be by merit only.

Gradually, as a result of Genghis Khan's policy, Mongol society came to resemble that of feudal Europe. The Noyans became great landowners; the commanders of the smaller units, the "Bagaturs" or brave warriors, had smaller estates; the rank and file were known as "Kharachu" or freemen, and owned small plots of grazing ground; lowest of all were the serfs who had been captured in battle.

The élite of the army was the Imperial Guard, totalling some ten thousand men. These were the best soldiers and officers picked from every military unit. In battle, they were used as shock troops, and fought with unbelievable ferocity. In peacetime,

Genghis Khan returning with his cavalry after a victorious raid.

over the empire to carry out the Khan's commands. In this way, they became of vital importance to both the army and the civil administration. They were a privileged caste who lived close to the Khan and received the best of everything. An ordinary ranking soldier in the guards had more prestige than even a general in the feudal army.

Genghis and his successors personally supervized the way the army was run, and inspected their troops before every campaign. If a soldier had lost any part of his equipment, he was severely punished. Much of the Mongols' military success was due to their remarkable discipline.

Weapons and armour

Mongol warriors wore leather jackets, trousers, long felt socks and high boots. Their armour was usually made out of oxhide strips, which were boiled and moulded to fit the shape of the wearer's body, and then lacquered to keep out the wet. Beneath this they wore silk shirts. Then, if a weapon entered their bodies, the silk was pressed into the wound and kept it clean and free from infection.

Later on, they made lamellar armour by sewing rectangular metal plates onto long leather tunics in overlapping rows. These long coats, or hauberks, reached almost to the ground, and were split up the front and back to make movement easier. Mongol helmets were simple, and their necks were protected by mail aventails, long flaps that reached down to their shoulders. Sometimes the helmets were topped by spikes onto which splendid horsehair plumes, jewelled feathers and even pennants were fixed.

The Mongols' favourite weapon was a short bow, which they fired from the saddle. Several strips of horn and wood were bound around a central core to give the bow flexibility and strength. The archers had to be strong men – a pull of as much as 166 pounds was needed just to bend the bows. But they were generally very accurate up to ranges of two or three hundred yards.

The Mongols carried their bows in oiled cases on their left hips, and their arrows in quivers on their right hips. This meant that they were able to "stand" in the stirrups, whip out their bows and arrows, and fire in one swift lithe movement to the left or right, to the front or rear. They also had longer bows for use in ground fighting.

At close quarters Mongols would cut their opponents down with curved sabres, which they

Above A Mongol on horseback.

Opposite Mongolian lamellar armour and, *far right*, a Mongol warrior in full battle gear.

40

LACED LAMELLAE BACK

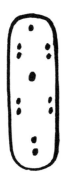

SINGLE UNLACED LAMELLAE

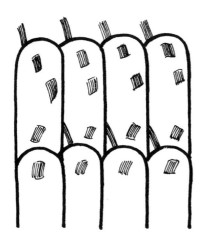

LACED LAMELLAE FRONT

carried in oiled leather cases behind their left shoulder. They also used long hooked lances to drag their enemies from the saddle. Although they carried shields whilst on guard duty, they scorned to use them in battle.

Every man also carried a short axe in his belt, a length of rope for tethering his horse, a tool kit containing wax, some spare bowstrings, files for sharpening arrowheads, and a needle and thread. In addition, he had a change of clothing, a supply of dried meat and milk, a leather bottle of koumiss or water, and a cooking pot.

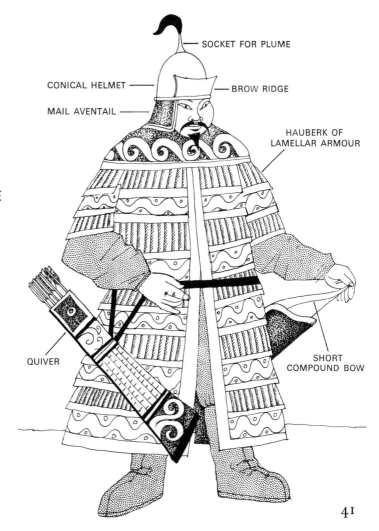

SOCKET FOR PLUME

CONICAL HELMET

MAIL AVENTAIL

BROW RIDGE

HAUBERK OF
LAMELLAR ARMOUR

QUIVER

SHORT
COMPOUND BOW

Men and horses

The Mongols were well equipped by nature for war. Their keen eyesight enabled them to see a man hiding behind a bush or rock up to four miles away. Their acute sense of smell helped them to discover recent camp sites. They were skilled trackers, and their knowledge of the climate, vegetation and habits of the steppe animals meant they could live off the country through which they travelled. Thanks to their remarkable powers of endurance, they could ride for days on end with little rest or food.

The horse was a Mongol's most prized possession. It provided him with almost everything he needed: food and drink, clothing and transport. Horses of every breed and colour were treasured, and white horses were considered sacred. Both men and women were accomplished riders, and young children were often tied to the backs of small ponies even before they could walk.

Mongol horses were truly remarkable animals. The Chinese claimed that they were sired by "heavenly stallions." They could cover long distances at a trot, and only needed short periods for grazing. The Mongols, of course, treated them with care, and did not use them for regular riding until they were three years old. On long journeys, a rider took three or four remounts, so that each horse could be rested in turn.

In battle, the horses wore armour. Their flanks, necks, backs and chests were protected by sheets of leather. Their saddles and stirrups, too, were solidly made, to make riding long distances more comfortable.

Horses were so important to the Mongols that they would scour the countryside they had invaded, looking for stallions to improve their breeding stock. On campaign, they would round up their enemies' herds in order to deprive them of cavalry mounts.

Below The Mongols were very fond of playing polo. It was good sport for them, since it increased the skills of both horse and rider.

Above Horse racing was also popular with the Mongols. These young jockeys are wearing special trousers to help them ride the horses without saddles.

Their own armies were accompanied by herds of remounts, many thousands in number. Each province of the Mongol empire had to provide a specified number of black, tawny, sorrel and skewbald horses as part of its tribute or tax.

Great occasions were marked by horse racing. Gaily dressed jockeys, boys ten or twelve years old, competed over various distances. The most popular event was the thirty mile race. The horses that won over these long distances, were greatly prized. Often they were worshipped by the common people, and, when they died, their skins and skulls were preserved and carried from place to place as sacred relics.

43

Military training

If an army is to be successful, it must function like a well-oiled machine. The Mongol Khans knew this, and they trained their troops to perfection.

Military training started in early childhood. Every Mongol boy was taught how to handle a bow and arrow from the age of three. As he grew up, he had to be prepared to defend himself and his camp at all times, and weapon training became part of his ordinary life. The importance of obedience was also impressed upon him.

Genghis Khan realized that hunting involved many of the skills and qualities necessary for a good soldier. In his Yasa, or code of laws, he stated: "When the Mongols are unoccupied with war, they shall devote themselves to hunting. The objective is not so much the chase itself as the training of warriors, who should acquire strength and become familiar with drawing the bow and other exercises." Hunting thus took the place of present day military manoeuvres.

At the beginning of winter, military units would come from all over the empire to gather at the Khan's headquarters. An area of several thousand square miles was chosen as the hunting ground. Then the regiments were deployed like an army, forming a centre, a left and a right wing. Once they had taken up their positions, the signal to advance was given and the regiments rode forward, driving the game before them. Over a period of one or two months, the columns gradually converged on each other until the animals were penned into a relatively small area. At this point, the Khan, who had been taking careful note of the proceedings, would join the army. He and the other royal princes entered the enclosure, which was full of plunging, terrified beasts, and started the shooting. The slaughter

went on for several days. Then a deputation of old men would intervene and beg the Khan to spare the remaining animals. After he had granted their request, the survivors were released and driven to the nearest pasture, so that they could then form the breeding stock for future generations. The dead animals were counted up and divided among the hunters, according to custom.

In this way, the troops were fed and trained at the same time.

Statue of a Mongol archer. Archery was so important to the Mongols' military tactics that boys started training in archery when they were only three years old.

45

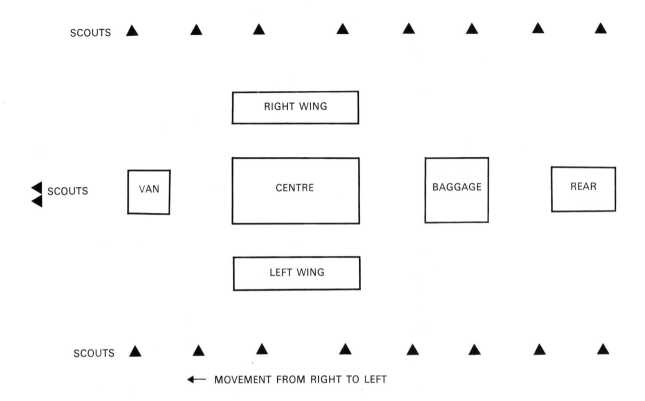

SCOUTS

RIGHT WING

SCOUTS | VAN | CENTRE | BAGGAGE | REAR

LEFT WING

SCOUTS

← MOVEMENT FROM RIGHT TO LEFT

Preparations for war

Every Mongol campaign was carefully planned. Scouts were sent ahead to reconnoitre the country through which the armies would pass, and to assess the strength of the enemy's defences. European merchants, who travelled back and forth between the Mediterranean world and China, also provided the Mongols with much useful information about what lay ahead. Since Genghis always treated them with respect, they were happy to co-operate with him. Then, when he was ready, the Khan would summon a meeting of all his officers to discuss the forthcoming campaign. After questioning the scouts and merchants, they would work out their strategy.

Left The deployment of a Mongol army on the march.

Below Genghis rests at a wayside inn. According to Marco Polo, Mongol inns were "large, handsome buildings, . . . well-furnished and hung with silk."

Once this was done, the chief Yurtchi, the quartermaster general, chose the best camping sites, and the routes along which the army could travel. His men then built up stocks of food and fodder along the road to the battle area.

Before the fighting started, the Mongols tried to divide and demoralize their enemies. Many of the countries they invaded were weakened by religious controversies. This gave the Mongols an advantage, since they were prepared to tolerate all religions. They also tried to win over the poor by promising them lower taxes, and terrifying them with stories of their atrocities. They were, in fact, masters of propaganda.

When the campaign got underway, the Mongol army of 160,000 men was divided into several separate columns, which followed completely different routes. Each column was made up of a vanguard, a left and right wing, and a centre, followed by a baggage train and rearguard. The army was accompanied by road managers to catalogue everything they captured, shamans to inspire and doctor the troops, and entertainers to while away the weary hours in camp.

In the wake of the army came the men of the Yam Department who built roads and inns in the country through which they had passed. According to Marco Polo, "there are post stations with accommodation for travellers at distances of 25 or 30 miles along every great road. These are large, handsome buildings; the apartments are well-furnished, hung with silk, and provided with everything suitable for persons of rank." Herds of horses and stores of provisions were kept at each inn. "Arrow" riders carried messages backwards and forwards between the commanders and the Great Khan. These riders were the best available, and messages could be carried from one end of the empire to the other with astonishing speed.

Tactics in war

The Mongols aimed to isolate, surround and annihilate their enemies in one swift movement. As soon as they sighted them, the Mongol light cavalry would attack, thundering right up to their opponents, stopping dead in a cloud of dust, and pouring volley after volley of arrows into their astonished foes. When the enemy advanced, the Mongols would turn their horses' heads and disappear in a flash. This tactic was repeated time and again.

If the enemy stood firm, the Mongols feigned flight, one of the oldest fighting tricks. Their cavalry would engage the enemy, and then withdraw in disorder. If their opponents pursued them, the Mongols swiftly reformed and counter-attacked at speed. Few armies could withstand such an onslaught.

Some of their opponents were made of sterner stuff and refused to be tricked into making mistakes. There was nothing for it then but for the Mongol army to fall back on traditional methods. The infantry was pushed forward with the prisoners-of-war in the front rank – if they tried to flee, they were killed. The movements of the various units were co-ordinated by flag and smoke signals. Once the enemy had been weakened, the Mongol heavy cavalry would attack. A great wall of horses charged down at a full gallop and smashed its way through the enemy's ranks, charging again and again until their opponents were destroyed.

Then the fleeing troops were pursued, relentlessly and without mercy. The infantry were ridden down and dispatched with the sword. The cavalry were overtaken, dragged from their saddles with hooked lances, and butchered. The Mongols were never satisfied with anything less then total victory.

When the Mongols themselves were surprised by

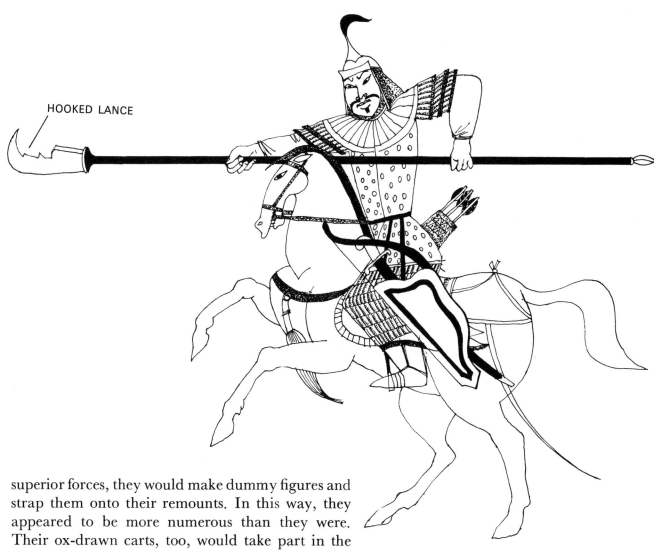

HOOKED LANCE

superior forces, they would make dummy figures and strap them onto their remounts. In this way, they appeared to be more numerous than they were. Their ox-drawn carts, too, would take part in the battle charges. Even the Mongol women fought, sorting through the piles of bodies and slitting the throats of the enemy wounded. In the last resort, the Mongols relied upon the speed and stamina of their horses to get them out of danger. They rarely failed to outrun and outlast their opponents. Then they would wait in a safe place until their enemies had passed by, before emerging once more to ravage the land.

In this way, they created a legend of invincibility.

Above The Mongol cavalry used hooked lances to deadly effect, dragging their enemies from their horses, and slaughtering them as they lay.

C

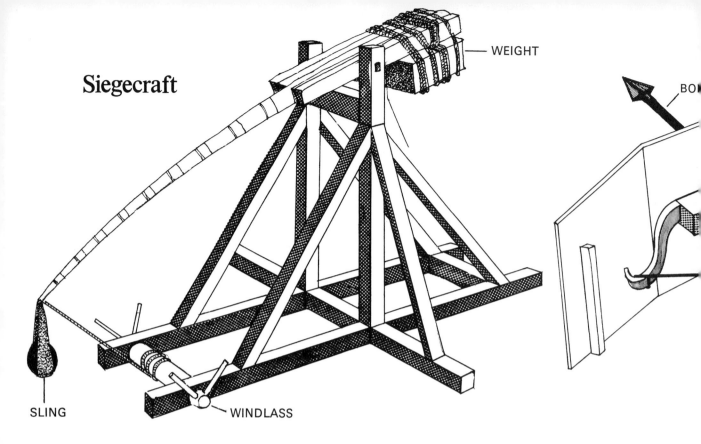

Siegecraft

WEIGHT

BO▮

SLING — WINDLASS

The Mongols developed effective techniques for dealing with fortified towns. If a long siege was expected, wooden walls were erected around the city to stop relief columns reaching it. Then, while the archers sniped at the defenders and kept them busy, Chinese engineers would bring up siege engines to pound at the walls.

These siege engines were of many different types. One of the commonest was the mangonel. It consisted of a pair of upright posts topped by a cross beam and set into a frame on wheels. A long whippy pole, secured to the axle by a web of ropes, was brought back and made fast with a release catch. Then the spoonbowl at the end of the pole was armed with a missile, and the web of ropes twisted tight by a capstan. When the safety-catch was released, the arm sprang up, struck the padded cross-beam and hurled the missile forwards. Mangonels fired rocks, or barrels of naptha, an in-

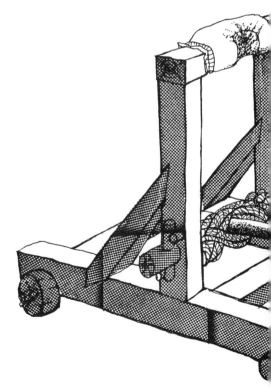

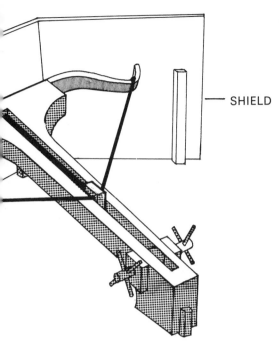

SHIELD

PADDED CROSS PIECE

CAPSTAN

WEB OF ROPES

WINDLASS

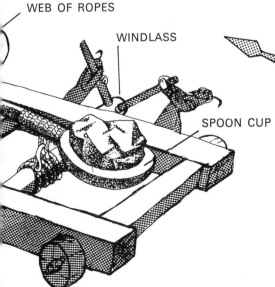

SPOON CUP

ROCKET

flammable substance made of sulphur and petroleum.

The trebuchet was much larger and more accurate. It consisted of two giant uprights, with a long arm pivoted between them; at one end was a sling, at the other a great weight. The arm was lowered by a windlass so the sling could be loaded. When the arm was released, the weight dropped, swinging up the sling and flinging the missile with great force towards its target.

The Chinese also knew how to make an incendiary material like gunpowder. They manufactured bombs for the Mongols who used to lob them into enemy cities with devastating effect. Rockets, bamboo tubes filled with this gunpowder substance and attached to long arrows, were also effective.

The ballista, a giant crossbow mounted on vertical stands, was another Mongol favourite. The bow was pivoted so that it could be raised or lowered as necessary. It fired enormous arrows, and iron bolts several feet long. The front was often hidden behind a large semi-circular shield, to protect the archers working it.

Battering rams and tunnelling were sometimes used to make the walls collapse. But the most characteristic Mongol habit during sieges was to chop up the people they had killed and throw their fat onto the enemy's buildings, which then burned furiously when ignited by fire-arrows.

Weapons of war made for the Mongols by Chinese engineers. *Opposite top* the trebuchet, *top left* the ballista, *left* a mangonel, and *below* a fire rocket.

51

4. Wars of expansion

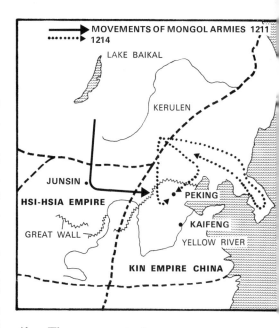

Above The movement of Genghis's armies against the Chinese in 1211 and 1214.

Now that he was master of a huge army, Genghis embarked upon a series of campaigns which amazed his contemporaries. His main objective was China, with its rich cities and flourishing agriculture. First of all, however, he had to conquer the Hsi-Hsia empire. In 1209, he descended on Junsin, the capital, like a thunderbolt. Soon he had forced its inhabitants to surrender and pay tribute to him.

Later, during the siege of Volotai, Genghis promised to withdraw if the governor of the town would hand over a thousand cats and ten thousand swallows. When the astonished governor complied, Genghis ordered his men to tie tufts of cotton to the cats' and swallows' tails, light them and set them free. The frightened animals and birds fled back to their homes, and soon had set the whole town ablaze.

Once Hsi-Hsia was his, Genghis set about attacking China in the spring of 1211. This was the most important campaign of his life. The Kin knew of his plans and prepared to defend their borders. However, they were completely routed. At a stroke, Genghis became master of all the lands bordering the Great Wall.

As news of this spread, the subject peoples of the Kin Empire rose in revolt to join Genghis. Soon, he had overrun the lands north of the Yellow River. But Genghis knew that he lacked the weapons and technical knowledge necessary to capture large, walled towns. He therefore made peace in 1214, in exchange for a Chinese princess whose dowry included a thousand boys and girls, three thousand horses, and much gold and silver.

This peace was really no more than an armed truce. Genghis drove off all the horses in northern

Right A Chinese town captured by Genghis Khan's army.

Below A Tartar warrior in the Chinese army.

China, so that the Kin could not rebuild their cavalry, and created a formidable siege train. When the Kin abandoned Peking, their northern troops mutinied and joined Genghis. By 1215, he was riding through the streets of Peking. Pushing home his advantage, he sent an army against Kaifeng. The Kin panicked and sued for peace. Their courage, however, returned when Genghis demanded all the lands north of the Yellow River. During the autumn, the Mongol army was defeated and had to retreat across the frozen Yellow River.

In 1216, Genghis returned to his tents on the Kerulen, leaving an army in China under the direction of Mukali, which continued to make slow but steady progress there.

Expansion westwards

Genghis returned home laden with booty. Soon he was famous for his hospitality, and the luxury of his court. A Chinese visitor reported a typical incident: "When the ambassador from Sung China failed to attend the Mongol games, Genghis sent for him and said: 'From the moment of your arrival in my empire, you became a member of my household. You must come and join us when we make merry or have a feast, a game of ball or hunt. Why wait for an invitation?' He then broke into laughter, imposed a penalty of six glasses of wine, and would only release the unfortunate ambassador at nightfall, when the latter had become quite drunk!"

Genghis now turned his eyes to the west where the Kara-Khitai empire lay. Here, an old enemy, Kuchluk the Naiman, had overthrown the native ruler and seized the throne for himself. Fortunately for Genghis, Kuchluk was unpopular with his new subjects. Taking advantage of their discontent, Genghis dispatched a strong army under Jebei to subdue the country. Jebei was an intelligent man. He set himself up as a liberator, and revolts occurred throughout Kara-Khitai. Kuchluk was swiftly defeated and killed. The Mongols continued to create a good impression there by allowing the Moslems freedom of worship, and by imposing only very light taxes.

Only the state of Khwarizm now lay between the Mongols and the Mediterranean. This included Turkestan, Afghanistan and Persia. Its ruler, Shah Muhammad, was a cruel despot who had lost the respect and devotion of most of his people. A Mongol embassy was sent to the border town of Otrar in Khwarizm, but it was massacred on the orders of the governor. To the Mongols, the person of an ambassa-

Genghis's army attacks the forces of Shah Muhammad, the ruler of Khwarizm.

dor was sacred. Genghis was furious at this outrage and sent another embassy to Samarkand, demanding redress. Not only did Muhammad refuse to punish the governor, he had the second ambassador executed as well. War was inevitable.

Genghis ordered recruits from every province in the Mongol empire for the coming campaign. Only Asha-Ganbo, the Tangut ruler, dared to refuse, saying: "If you haven't enough troops, you are not fit to be Khan." Genghis vowed vengeance against him: "If the Spirit of Heaven preserves me, I will march against you on my return from Khwarizm." For the time being, however, he ignored the Tangut and prepared for the invasion of the west.

55

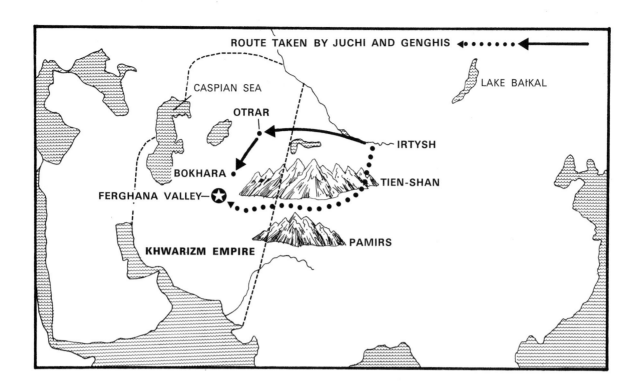

ROUTE TAKEN BY JUCHI AND GENGHIS ◄••••••◄━━━━

LAKE BAIKAL

CASPIAN SEA

OTRAR

IRTYSH

TIEN-SHAN

BOKHARA

FERGHANA VALLEY—

PAMIRS

KHWARIZM EMPIRE

Juchi's raid

In the summer of 1219, Genghis assembled his army beside the River Irtysh. While he was making his final preparations, he sent his eldest son, Juchi, to search for an eastern route into Khwarizm. Juchi and his band had to struggle for many days through deep snow in the passes of the Pamirs and Tien-Shan mountains. They wrapped their horses' legs in yak skins to prevent them freezing, and kept themselves alive by opening the veins in their horses' necks and drinking their hot blood. A trail of bones marked their progress as the ravenous Mongols ate the flesh of dead comrades. At last, after unspeakable hardships, they entered the lovely valley of Ferghana. Before they could recover their strength, however, Shah Muhammad arrived with his troops. Juchi's counsellors advised him to withdraw but the young man replied: "How could I ever face my father if I ran away?"

Routes taken by the Mongol armies in Genghis's victorious campaign against Khwarizm.

56

Right To protect their horses from the appalling cold, Juchi's men wrapped yak skins round the horses' legs.

Muhammad launched his army against the Mongols to the harsh snarling of war trumpets and the clash of cymbals, but without success. The Mongols scattered, wheeled, regrouped and attacked again and again with bewildering speed. The battle swung back and forth until nightfall. By morning, the Mongols had disappeared, leaving only corpses on the battlefield. The Shah dared not follow them up into the mountains.

Now, Genghis launched the main attack. His sons Jagatai and Ogedai were sent to capture Otrar. The city held out for five months before surrendering to the furious Mongols. The governor was captured and sent to the Khan, who had molten silver poured into his eyes and ears before torturing him to death.

Genghis advanced to Bokhara. The city surrendered without a siege except for the gallant soldiers of the citadel, who held out for twelve days before they were overwhelmed and massacred. The Khan demanded lists of all the wealthy men in the city, and made them hand over their riches. The ordinary people were driven out into the wilderness with nothing but the clothes they wore. During the subsequent orgy of pillaging, the beautiful city was set on fire and burned to the ground.

A Moslem priest tried to reconcile his people to their fate, saying: "Be silent and do what you are bidden. Things may go worse with us, for the wrath of God has overtaken us." This was just what Genghis wanted them to believe.

57

The end of Shah Muhammad

From Bokhara, Genghis made his way to Samarkand, the centre of the eastern Moslem world. It was a beautiful city, with a population of half a million, rich markets, great libraries and magnificent palaces. Samarkand only held out for five days, but Genghis exacted a cruel revenge. Only the Moslem priests were safe from Mongol troops who looted the city and razed its walls to the ground. The entire garrison was put to the sword. This was not so much wanton cruelty as a cold-blooded attempt to terrify the garrisons in other towns into instant submission.

At Nishapur, all the inhabitants were slaughtered and their heads cut off. The skulls of the men, women and children were piled into separate pyramids; even the dogs and cats were killed. Nishapur ceased to exist.

After their victories in Khwarizm, Genghis sent his generals Jebei and Subodai across the Caucasus to Russia.

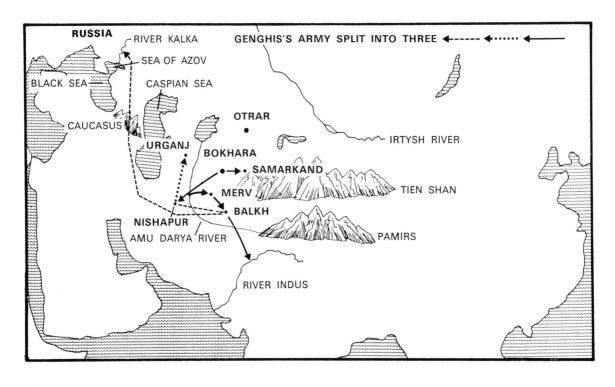

Below right Confrontation
between the Mongol and the
Persian armies.

At this point, Genghis heard that Shah
Muhammad had fled across the Amu Darya to
Balkh, where he was trying to raise new forces.
Genghis sent his generals Jebei and Subodai swiftly
after him, but he need not have worried – the Shah
fled to an island in the Caspian Sea where he died
miserably soon after. Undismayed, Jebei and Subodai
crossed the Caucasus mountains and invaded
southern Russia, defeating a Christian force at
the battle of the River Kalka, near the Sea of
Azov.

Meanwhile, Genghis continued his triumphant
progress through Khwarizm, capturing town after
town with his new siege engines. He spent the winter
of 1220–1 by the river Amu Darya. The following
year, his sons Juchi and Jagatai went off to conquer
Urganj, the capital of Khwarizm. However, they
quarrelled so violently that Genghis had to put
their younger brother, Ogedai, in charge of the army.

The Khan himself followed Muhammad's son,
Jelal-ud-din, down to the south, capturing the rich
cities of Merv and Balkh on the way. Jelal retreated
further southwards until he was finally trapped by
the River Indus behind him. After a closely fought
battle, the Mongols were victorious. Rather than
allow his mother, wives and children to fall into
Mongol hands, Jelal had them thrown into the river
and drowned. Then he galloped his horse to the edge
of a sixty-foot cliff and flung himself into the Indus.
Bearing his banner before him he started to swim.
Genghis applauded his courage and forbade his
troops to shoot at him: "Let him live and fight
another day!"

The last years of Genghis Khan

By this time, Genghis longed to return to his own lands. At first he planned to make his way home through India and Tibet, but these countries were spared this experience by the intervention of the shamans, who told the Khan that the time was unfavourable. They were right – news soon reached Genghis that the Tanguts had risen in revolt.

As the Khan rode in the cool shadow of the Hindu Kush mountains, he spent many hours discussing religion with a learned Chinese monk called Ch'ang Ch'un. At the end of their conversations, Genghis announced: "Ch'ang Ch'un has thrice explained to me how to preserve life, and I have committed his words to memory." Nevertheless, he remained true to his belief in the Great Spirit of the Sky who had raised him so high.

The winter was spent in Samarkand. But in January, 1223, Genghis was on the move again. While hunting wild boar along the banks of the Tashkent river, he was thrown from his horse and was nearly killed by the furious animal. The Khan remarked ruefully: "We Mongols are accustomed to shoot from the saddle from our earliest years, and find it hard to lose the habit."

Advancing eastwards, Genghis spent the summer in the neighbourhood of the River Irtysh, where he taught his grandsons Kublai and Hulagu to hunt. He reached his homelands in 1225.

In 1226, Genghis collected his armies together for the last time and led an expedition against the Tangut. Even though he was an old man of seventy-two, he insisted on taking command himself. The Tangut resisted stubbornly, but the Mongols captured town after town. As Genghis lay before the city of Ning-Hia, he heard that his eldest son Juchi had died. Soon he felt the approach of death him-

On his death bed, Genghis gave each of his sons an arrow, saying "All power is weak, unless it is united."

self. After giving his generals their instructions for the completion of the campaign, he named Ogedai as his successor. Then, calling all his sons and grandsons to him, he said: "With Heaven's help, I have conquered for you a large empire, but my life was too short to achieve the conquest of the whole world. That task is left to you." He was buried on the slopes of Mount Burkan-Kaldun where his career had begun so many years before.

5. The conquest of the world

In the spring of 1227, the Great Kuriltai of Mongol chieftains assembled to elect Ogedai Khan as Genghis had wished. Ogedai was very different from his father. Although a drunkard and a womanizer he had proved himself a good soldier and able administrator. On coming to the throne, he sent armies off in every direction.

Tolui, Genghis's youngest son, led the main army against the Kin Chinese. To ensure success, the Mongols made an alliance with the southern Chinese, or Sung, promising them the province of Honan. On Tolui's death, the great general,

Subodai, conducted another brilliant campaign. The Kin capital, Kaifeng, was besieged for a whole year. When it was clear that its defenders would have to surrender, the old general wrote to Ogedai promising to destroy the city, and to slaughter its two million inhabitants, just as Genghis would have liked. However, this was not to be. Ogedai had been listening to his advisers, who counselled a change of policy. The Great Khan therefore commanded Subodai to spare the Chinese, and to treat them with respect. The conquest of Kin China was finally completed after twenty-four years of war. The last Kin emperor committed suicide, and Ogedai ruled in his place. The Great Khan then turned south, and ordered his generals to prepare to attack the Sung.

Meanwhile, another Mongol army headed for Persia, where Jelal-ud-din had established himself as sultan. Like his father Muhammad before him, Jelal was interfering in his neighbours' affairs, and was caught off guard by the Mongol onslaught. He failed to raise an army, and was betrayed by his own minister before managing to escape once more. He made his way into the Kurdistan mountains, but here his adventures ended miserably – he was murdered by a band of robbers who did not even know who their victim was.

More ambitious than either of these campaigns was Ogedai's determination to conquer Europe. The Mongols knew little about this area but this only served to make it more attractive to them. A magnificent army was assembled, containing recruits from every province in the empire. Its nominal leader was the wily and experienced Batu, the eldest son of Juchi, but the brains behind the attack were those of the old general Subodai. In this army marched most of Genghis's descendants, including Ogedai's sons, Kuyuk and Kaidan, and Tolui's son Mangu.

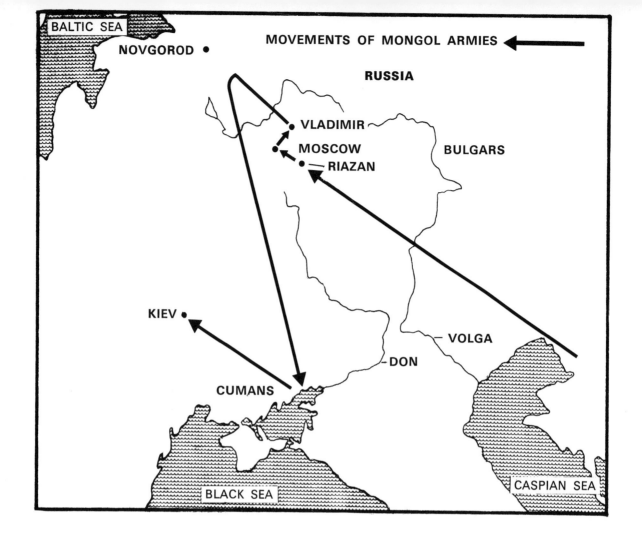

The attack on Russia

The campaign opened in 1236 with the conquest of the Bulgars, Cumans and other tribes of the lower Don and Volga region. Throughout the following summer, the prisoners-of-war were taught to fight in Mongol fashion. And then, in December, the great army stole across the frozen Volga.

It was the old general Subodai who counselled an attack on northern Russia in the depth of winter. Unlike the French under Napoleon in 1812, or the Germans under Hitler in 1942, the Mongols

64

Opposite The route taken by the Mongol armies in their attack on Russia.

Below Typical Russian warriors.

were not upset by the bitter Russian cold. They were used to such conditions at home in Mongolia. Moreover, in winter most of the Russian rivers and lakes were frozen which made them easy to cross.

Although the Russians had heard of the Mongols' attack against the Bulgars, they were not expecting any trouble themselves, and were taken completely by surprise. The Mongols captured Riazan on 21st December, 1237, and left "no eyes open to weep for the dead." Then they advanced on Moscow, in those days a small and insignificant town. According to the Russian chroniclers, "the men of Moscow ran away before the barbarians came in sight." The Russian Grand Duke Yuri II, however, decided to give battle. He left a sizeable garrison in his capital, Vladimir, and set up his banner on the banks of the River Sit.

As soon as the Russian soldiers had disappeared from sight, Subodai attacked Vladimir. After six days, the city was captured and all its inhabitants, including the Grand Duke's family, were slain. Next, Subodai divided his army up into columns, and fell upon the unhappy Grand Duke from all sides. Yuri and most of his men perished.

The Mongols then sped towards Novgorod, but were halted by the spring thaw, which turned the country into a quagmire. They turned back and carried fire and sword through southern Russia. On reaching the lower Don basin, they stopped to rest, and remained there for the whole of 1239, strengthening their hold over the Cumans.

Then, refreshed and reinforced, they plunged back into Russia in 1240 and captured the magnificent city of Kiev, with its sparkling golden domes and glowing white walls. The slaughter was so great that, five years later, the plain was still covered with the bones of the slain. Less than two hundred houses remained standing in the once large and prosperous town.

The campaign in Eastern Europe

Most of the Russian princes surrendered to the victorious Mongols. Batu then divided his army up into columns again, and sent them off in different directions.

Kaidan led his mounted hordes into Poland where on, 24th March, 1241, the ancient city of Cracow was entirely destroyed. Duke Henry of Silesia assembled all available forces at Liegnitz. Breaking with tradition, the Mongols attacked in silence, pouring a deadly hail of arrows into the densely packed ranks of heavily armoured knights. Stung to fury, they attacked vigorously, brushing the nomads aside. Intoxicated with their success, they chased the fleeing Mongols and fell into an ambush. Few of them emerged from it alive. The survivors found

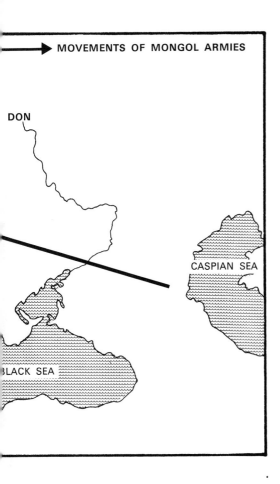

MOVEMENTS OF MONGOL ARMIES

DON

CASPIAN SEA

BLACK SEA

Above The Mongol armies threaten to overrun Europe.

Opposite The victorious Mongol armies left in their wake a trail of devastated towns.

themselves struggling in thick, acrid smoke from the Mongol fires, and fled. This is one of the first recorded uses of a smoke-screen to confuse the enemy. Between thirty and forty thousand men were killed. The Mongols cut off the right ears of the dead, and filled seven large sacks with them.

Another wing of the Mongol army entered Hungary, and ravaged the land around Budapest. King Bela of Hungary drew up his army on the plain of Mohi, beside the River Sajo. During the night, the Mongols brought up their siege weapons and lobbed fire-bombs into the Hungarian camp, causing great panic. In the morning, the Hungarians discovered that a Mongol force had swum the river, and hurled themselves on their foe. Meanwhile, another group of Mongols forded the river unseen, and attacked their rear. Driven back into their camp, they fought bravely. Then they noticed a gap in the ring of Mongols surrounding them. Seizing their opportunity, the Hungarians rushed through this narrow channel, only to find their enemies waiting for them at the end. Once again, most of the Europeans were butchered, although King Bela himself managed to escape.

In a little less than a month, the entire countryside from the Baltic to the Danube had been occupied and looted by the Mongols. Panic seized the nations of Europe. Where would they strike next? The Mongols rested throughout the summer and autumn. Then, in December 1241, they crossed the frozen Danube. One army entered Dalmatia, another subdued Hungary, and a third advanced to within a few miles of Vienna. Europe was doomed. But suddenly the Mongols turned, and went back the way they had come. Europe was saved. But why?

The crisis

In faraway Karakorum, the Mongol capital, Ogedai had died. Batu and other descendants of Genghis Khan all hoped to succeed him. While the members of the "Golden Family" intrigued against each other, Ogedai's widow, Turakina, ruled as regent between 1242 and 1246. Eventually, she succeeded in getting her eldest son, Kuyuk, elected Khan. He, however, had a reputation for occupying himself "with goblets of wine and lovely fair cheeked creatures."

At this time, an envoy, John of Plano Carpini, arrived from Pope Innocent IV. He described Kuyuk's enthronement: "We saw a tent of fine white cloth. Around it had been erected a wooden palisade on which various designs had been painted. On the first day, they all dressed in white velvet, on the second in scarlet, on the third in blue and on the fourth in the finest brocade. It was marvellous to behold how many gifts were presented by the ambassadors – silk, brocade, golden girdles, choice furs, and a little sunshade decorated with precious stones."

The Pope called on the Khan to end the attack against Europe and become a Christian. In reply, Kuyuk insisted that the Pope and the kings of Europe come to Karakorum and do homage to "the Khan of all the peoples of the earth."

However, Kuyuk died, probably poisoned, before he could carry out any of his plans, and the struggle for the throne started again. Kuyuk's widow, Katum Ogul-Gamish, was regent between 1248 and 1251. She was a greedy and superstitious woman, and earned the hatred of her relatives by experimenting with black magic. Eventually, Tolui's eldest son, Mangu, was elected Khan. As soon as he was on

68

The coronation of Kuyuk Khan. John of Plano Carpini, an envoy of the Pope, was most impressed by the richness of the clothes worn at the ceremony, and the sumptuous gifts brought to the new Khan.

the throne, he had all the most ambitious members of his family murdered, including Katum Ogul-Gamish.

The western powers still hoped to win the support of the Mongols. King Louis IX of France sent his envoy, William of Rubruck, to Karakorum where he was received by the Khan in 1255. "The Emperor," he wrote, "was seated on a couch dressed in a glossy, spotted skin like a seal's. He is a little man of forty-five years of age. A young wife reclined beside him and a very ugly girl called Cirina sat with the other children on another couch." The Khan listened to Louis IX's message, but insisted that the French King would have to do homage before he would consider an alliance.

69

Triumphal progress

While William of Rubruck was talking with the Khan, a Mongol army was being assembled for the invasion of the Near East. Four thousand Chinese technicians were recruited to work the siege engines. Parties of engineers were sent ahead to build or repair the bridges over the great rivers. Stores of food and drink were set up along the route. Fodder and grazing land was reserved for the horses.

Mangu gave his brother Hulagu command of this expedition. Hulagu was a thirty-seven year old epileptic, but he was an able and experienced soldier. The army crossed the Amu Darya early in 1256, and set about exterminating a band of dangerous Moslem fanatics, called the Assassins. These religious murderers had built a series of almost impregnable fortresses in the mountains of

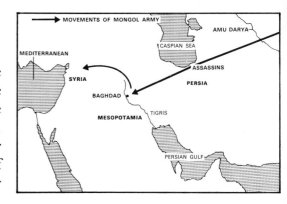

Above The Mongol army moves towards the Mediterranean.

Below Hulagu, grandson of Genghis Khan, chases his defeated enemies to their death.

northern Persia, and had successfully defied many formidable enemies, including the great Saladin. Their reputation and mountain strongholds did not protect them from the Mongols, who captured their hide-outs with ease, and put their defenders to the sword.

Next, they descended into Mesopotamia, and besieged the magnificent city of Baghdad. After a lengthy siege, its ruler, the Caliph Mustasin, was forced to surrender. The petrified Caliph emerged from the city and knelt before the cold impassive Hulagu, who demanded to know where his treasures were buried. As soon as the Caliph had disclosed their hiding places, the Mongol signalled to his men who rushed in and massacred the Caliph and his attendants. The townspeople were so horrified by this that they made no effort to defend themselves. 800,000 men, women and children were killed. The blood letting continued for forty days, until Hulagu himself was forced to withdraw from the neighbourhood of the city by the appalling, all-pervading smell of putrefaction. The city was left a smouldering ruin, its palaces, mosques, colleges and libraries gutted.

As Hulagu made his triumphal progress through Syria, one man was foolish enough to defy him. This man, a Moslem prince called al-Kamil, had the Khan's envoy seized and crucified. Hulagu's revenge was horrific. When the Moslem's castle fell at last, he forced the wretched man to cut off his own flesh and eat it until death released him from his agony.

At this point, Hulagu was joined by Louis IX's Crusaders, who saw the Mongols as the instruments of God sent to destroy the Moslems.

Entertainments held in honour of Hulagu, after his victorious campaigns in Syria and Mesopotamia.

71

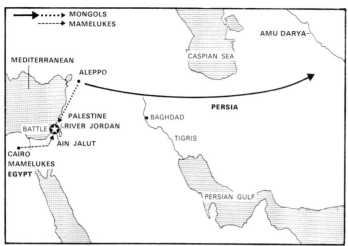

The field of Ain Jalut

Aleppo fell to these strange allies, the Mongols and the Crusaders, in January 1260. It seemed that Jerusalem and Cairo would suffer a similar fate. The Moslem faith would be destroyed and the Holy Lands restored to the Christians. It was at this crucial juncture that the Emperor Mangu died, faraway in Szechwan, China. Hulagu had to return with most of his troops to Persia, so that he could keep in touch with events at home. However, he ordered his second-in-command, Kitboga, to continue the campaign. And, before leaving Aleppo, Hulagu delivered an ultimatum to the Sultan of Egypt: "You have heard how we have conquered a vast empire and have purified the earth and slaughtered a great part of its inhabitants. It is for you to flee and for us to pursue."

Egypt was a rich and mighty country. Her capital, Cairo, was one of the finest cities in the world. She was defended by an army of slaves, the Mamelukes, who had seized control in 1250 and

The Egyptian Mamelukes, as depicted *left* in a late eighteenth-century engraving, defeated the Mongols at the Battle of Ain Jalut (*see opposite*). This ended Mongol expansion towards the Mediterranean.

ruled until 1517. Their military training, arms and discipline were quite equal to those of the Mongols'. Kutuz, the Egyptian Sultan, had the Mongol envoys executed, and their heads displayed in all four quarters of Cairo. Then he collected a great army, and set out to destroy the Mongols.

On 3rd September, 1260, he confronted Kitboga at Ain Jalut (Goliath's Spring) near the River Jordan in Palestine. The Mongols, greatly outnumbered, were easily defeated. The unfortunate Kitboga was led captive before the Sultan, but he remained defiant to the end: "Do not be elated by your temporary success," he told Kutuz. "If I die, it is God's will, not yours. When the news of my death reaches Hulagu Khan, his wrath will boil over like an angry sea. From Azerbaijan to the gates of Egypt, the whole land will be trampled under the hooves of the Mongol horses. Hulagu has 300,000 warriors equal to me. My death will only reduce them by one!" He was beheaded.

Kitboga's brave words were not realized, however. Hulagu soon quarrelled with his cousin Berke, the Khan of the Golden Horde, who ruled Russia. He needed all the troops he had to defend the Caucasus frontier. The battle of Ain Jalut thus ended Mongol expansion towards the Mediterranean. It also sealed the fate of the crusading states, which ceased to exist after 1291.

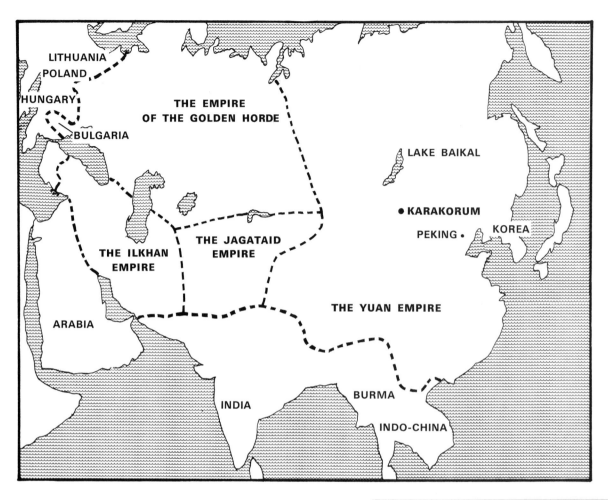

The succession problem

While Hulagu was conquering the Near East, his brother Kublai was leading a successful campaign in southern China. Mangu Khan was so jealous of his younger brother's success that he recalled him to Karakorum in 1257, and ordered an inquiry into his conduct of the war in China. Wisely, Kublai obeyed his brother and did everything he asked. But Mangu remained suspicious, and soon took command of the Mongol army in China. This was a fatal

Opposite As Genghis had feared, the vast area controlled by the Mongols soon split up into different empires.

Below The Khan of the Golden Horde receives homage from the Russian princes.

decision – the Emperor caught dysentery while on campaign and died in August, 1259.

For once it seemed that there would be no struggle for the throne since Kublai was the obvious successor. However, at the last moment, his younger brother, Arik-Buka, put himself forward too as a candidate. Before Kublai could reach Karakorum, Arik-Buka had convened a Kuriltai, which elected him Khan. When Kublai heard what his brother had done, he called a Kuriltai of his own, and was elected Khan as well. Since neither of the two brothers would give way, war broke out between them. Kublai soon drove his brother out of Mongolia, and Arik-Buka was still retreating at the time of his death, in 1264.

By this time, it was obvious that the Mongol Empire was breaking up into smaller units. Hulagu and his descendants ruled over Persia as Ilkhans, Jagatai's descendants reigned in Turkestan, and the sons of Batu controlled Russia as Khans of the Golden Horde. Kublai was recognized by them all as the Great Khan, but he left the western half of his Empire in their hands.

In 1267, Kublai set out to conquer Sung China once more. He made Peking his capital, and adopted a Chinese name, Yuan, for his family. He treated the Chinese well, and listened to their advice. This policy paid off. When the Dowager Sung Empress and her son were captured in 1276, the boy renounced his claim to the throne, and Kublai became Emperor of the whole of China.

Many Mongols, however, objected to Kublai's obsession with China, and there was a revolt under Ogedai's grandson, Kaidu. Kublai, realizing the danger, sent Bayan, his best general, to Mongolia, where he succeeded in regaining Karakorum. But as Kublai was not prepared to station most of his troops in the north, Central Mongolia soon became virtually independent, Kublai was not dismayed – he felt that China was his home.

6. Kublai Khan

"Kublai Khan is of middle height, neither tall nor short," wrote Marco Polo, a merchant from Venice who lived in Mongol China between 1275 and 1291. "His limbs are well-shaped, and his body is well-proportioned. His complexion is fair, and occasionally flushes red like the bright tint of a rose. His eyes are black and handsome, his nose well-shaped and prominent."

The new Emperor of China became a Buddhist, and built a great temple in honour of his ancestors. He enclosed his new capital, Cambulac, with high walls, and built a large ornamental lake, an observatory and huge barracks for his regiments of Guards. According to Marco Polo, "the walls of the Imperial palace are plated with gold and silver, and adorned with figures of dragons, beasts and birds." Six thousand people could dine at once in the great banqueting hall. The Emperor was waited on by nobles who "covered their mouths with their napkins so their breath may not taint his food and drink. When the Khan drinks, the musicians play and all the lords and people bow down before him." However, Kublai did not forget his humble origins. He would take his sons to a secret part of the Royal Park, which was planted with steppe grass, and remind them: "This is your true heritage. From this have you come."

The Emperor's main relaxation was hunting – with hounds, hawks or leopards. "He is carried upon the backs of four elephants in a fine timber howdah [canopied seat], which is plated with gold inside and covered with skins outside."

Kublai was also a great collector. A huge ruby from Siam "as big as a man's clenched fist," cunningly carved ivories, beautiful jade ornaments and

Kublai Khan (*opposite*), the first Mongol Emperor of all China, thoroughly enjoyed hunting (*see below*). His howdah was carried on four elephants, and plated with gold inside.

pearls "as large as birds' eggs" were stored in his treasury. He was a sensual man. In the Imperial harem were beautiful girls who "have sweet breath, sleep without snoring and are round and supple." His four wives had separate households. They were treated with great respect, and, between them, gave the Emperor more than twenty children.

Kublai was a great patron of the arts. He made his court a centre of learning, and welcomed painters, poets, architects and engineers from all over the world. He revised the calendar, and ordered dictionaries to be compiled. He commissioned books on farming and silk manufacture, and also encouraged the writing of novels and plays.

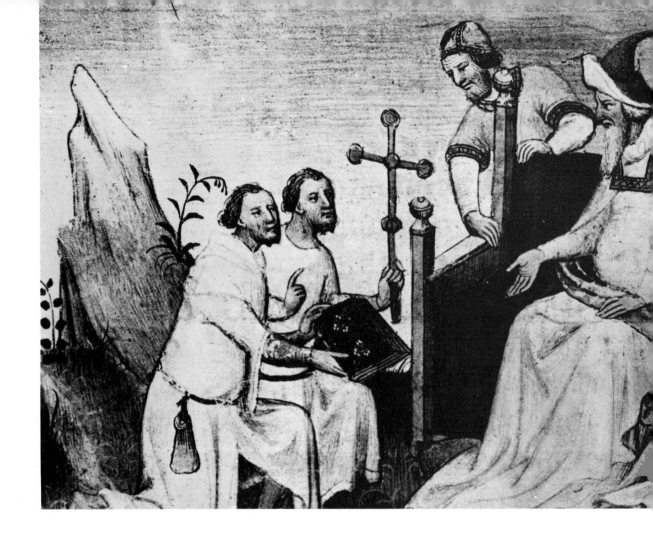

Mongol China

Kublai was determined to improve conditions in China. Three spectres – plague, drought and famine – had for centuries stalked the Chinese. The Emperor therefore set up hospitals in every province to care for the sick. Water conservation schemes were put in hand along the mighty rivers. Stores of grain were kept for use in times of emergency.

The Emperor encouraged commerce. He restarted work on the Grand Canal between the Yellow River and the Yangtse-Kiang. The great waterways teemed with traders. 200,000 cargo ships visited

The Venetian explorer
Marco Polo being received
by Kublai Khan.

Chinese ports every year, carrying black pepper, white walnuts and cloves from Java; ginger, cotton and muslins from Ceylon; and diamonds and pearls from India. More and more caravans followed the overland route to the West.

Kublai issued paper money whose value was fixed by law. Marco Polo observed that "these pieces of paper are printed with as much care as if they were actually pure gold or silver. On every piece officials write their names. Then, the chief officer puts red vermilion on the State seal, and stamps it on the paper. The money is then authenticated. Anybody forging it is put to death."

During the Emperor's reign, the Chinese burnt "black stones" (coal) as fuel, and collected a black liquid (oil) that welled up out of the earth to use in their flame-throwers. Chinese sailors threaded their way through fogs and dark nights by using a bamboo box containing a magnetized needle floating in water – the first compass.

An army of civil servants was required to carry out the Emperor's commands. Inevitably, corruption was widespread and difficult to detect, even though Kublai appointed special officers called Censors to ferret out the guilty. The most corrupt of all his servants was his chief minister, a Persian named Ahmed. After a time, the Chinese could stand it no longer – a group of them bluffed their way into the Imperial palace and murdered Ahmed. When he learned about his chief minister's wickedness, Kublai ordered Ahmed's sons to be flayed alive, and tossed their father's body into the street for the dogs to devour.

Such was Imperial justice that, as a Chinese chronicler expressed it, "a maiden bearing a nugget of gold could wander safely throughout the realm." He continued: "Kublai Khan must be regarded as one of the greatest rulers that ever lived, since his achievements are lasting."

The last of the Great Ones

Towards the end of his reign, Kublai was worshipped
like a god. His nobles bowed down before him, and
set up altars in his honour. His growing complacency,
however, was shattered by the news that the Manchus
were invading northern China. With a vigour that
surprised Marco Polo, he collected his army and
made his way north by forced marches. He reached
the Manchu camp near the Liao river in the early
hours of the morning, and the attack was launched
to the sound of Mongol wardrums, and the deafening
explosions of fire-bombs. Kublai was crippled with
gout, but he directed the battle himself from his bed,

and completely vanquished the Manchus.

Freed from this menace, he sent his armies to conquer the lost provinces of the Chinese empire. Time and again, the Mongols threw themselves into the jungles of Tong-king, and fought with people who disappeared into the shadows, and shot at them with poisoned arrows. In the end, their courage was rewarded – the native princes submitted to Kublai, and sent him a statue of pure gold as tribute. When the King of Annam then refused to allow the Mongols to pass through his realm, his lands were invaded and devastated. Three bloody wars were fought in Burma, where the Mongols had to deal with elephant cavalry. Kublai's soldiers also fought in Siam, in Hindustan beyond the Ganges, and in the jungles of Java. His fleets ravaged the shores of Malaya and the Philippines. The casualty lists grew longer and longer, but the Emperor remained unmoved.

In 1291, lured by the hope of rich booty, he sent a great armada of Mongols, Chinese and Koreans across the sea to Japan. But, on landing, they found themselves faced by the fierce samurai, experts in the use of long sword and bow, who knew no fear. Almost at once, a typhoon, the Japanese called it the "Kamikaze" or "Divine Wind," destroyed the Mongol fleet and left them stranded, facing a merciless foe. The Mongols were put to death, the Chinese and Koreans were enslaved. To the day of his death, Kublai dreamed of revenge, but this was not to be.

In 1294, Kublai Khan died, in the eightieth year of his life and the thirty-fifth of his reign. His body was carried back to Mongolia, where it was buried beside those of his ancestors.

Opposite Two Japanese warriors. The Mongols suffered a severe defeat at the hands of the fearless Samurai.

Below The areas of the Far East controlled by Kublai Khan.

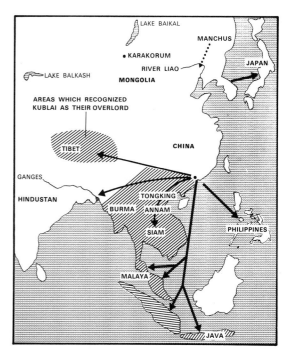

81

7. The Mongol legacy

After the death of Kublai Khan, the arrogant behaviour of the Mongol nobles aroused great anger amongst the Chinese, who were excluded from government service and forbidden to bear arms. The Mongols hunted over farm lands, and forced the Chinese to help them. This aroused great anger amongst the peasants. Mongol relations with Chinese townspeople were not as bad until peasant revolts cut off food supplies. Trade was reduced, and the paper money became valueless. For a time, the Chinese ruling class supported the Mongols, because they feared the peasants themselves. Gradually, however, they too turned against their overlords, and supported a great rebel leader called Chu Yuan-chang (1328–98). He drove the Mongols out of China, and founded the Ming dynasty.

The effect of Mongol rule on China is hard to determine. Because the Chinese ruling classes were excluded from government, they turned their attention to art and literature – the output of plays and novels increased considerably. Thanks to the increased opportunities for trade offered by the Mongol empire, Chinese merchants prospered too. Unfortunately, the Mongols themselves gained little from their contact with Chinese culture, and most of them remained uninterested in the arts.

The descendants of Jagatai ruled Central Asia for several generations and attempted to conquer India. Gradually they intermarried with the local people, and ceased to exist as a separate nation. When the royal family died out, a fierce Turk called Tamerlane (1336–1405) seized power, and created a huge empire of his own.

Hulagu's heirs reigned in Persia for many years. They approached the popes, and the kings of

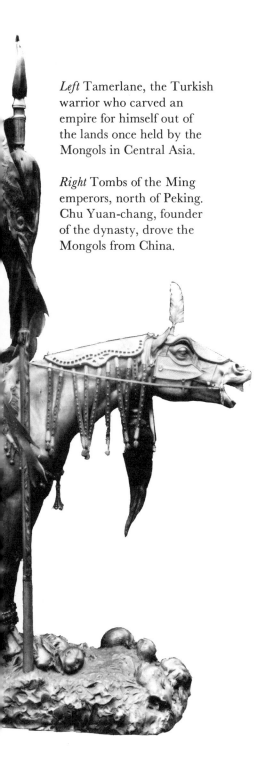

Left Tamerlane, the Turkish warrior who carved an empire for himself out of the lands once held by the Mongols in Central Asia.

Right Tombs of the Ming emperors, north of Peking. Chu Yuan-chang, founder of the dynasty, drove the Mongols from China.

Western Europe, in the hope of reviving the old alliance against the Egyptian Mamelukes, but with little success – the days of the crusades were over. Like their relatives in Central Asia, the Ilkhans were soon indistinguishable from the Persians among whom they lived. They became Moslems, and adopted the native language and customs. Their main influence on the area was to introduce certain new forms of armour, and methods of warfare. They, on the other hand, enjoyed the ancient culture of Persia, and became great patrons of the arts. The royal family came to an end in 1335.

The Mongols in Russia

The Mongols ruled Russia for over two centuries, and had a great influence on the development of the country. They devastated the cities so thoroughly that many Russians returned to the countryside, and learning and craftsmanship declined. On the other hand, the Russian Orthodox Church flourished since it was treated with respect by the Mongols, and it acquired large estates.

Russia was cut off from Western Europe, and her way of life became orientalized. Russian women wore the veil, and lived in seclusion. The Mongol knout, a three-stringed whip made out of rawhide, became a symbol of oppression. Mongol tortures were adopted by the Russians. Prisoners-of-war were thrashed with the knout to make them divulge military secrets. If this failed, the victim was placed on a rack where his arms and legs were dislocated, causing terrible pain. Finally, his head was shaved so that a naked flame could be played over it, or boiling water dropped on it. These tortures were commonly used in Russia until the end of the eighteenth century, and the knout lasted a great deal longer.

As a result of the Mongol conquest, the town of Vladimir ceased to dominate Russia. Instead, gradually, the small town of Moscow rose in importance – one of Moscow's Grand Dukes managed to become the chief tax-collector for the Mongols. His name was Ivan Kalita or Ivan "Money-Bags" (1328–40). Moscow's pre-eminence was accepted, and it became the centre of government for the whole country.

The Mongols influenced Russian attitudes towards government too. Impressed by the power of the Mongol Khans, Russian rulers insisted on being

Left Ivan the Terrible, ruler
of Moscow, crushed the
Mongol Khanates of
Kazan in 1552 and
Astrakhan in 1556.

autocrats, and demanded unlimited power over their
subjects.

Gradually, the unity of the Golden Horde declined,
until it split up into four smaller units: the Khanates
of Kazan, Astrakhan, Siberia and the Crimea. As
the Mongols weakened, the Russians took courage
and attacked them. One of Moscow's greatest rulers,
Ivan the Terrible (1533–84), dealt them two crushing
blows. In 1552, he captured Kazan and, four years
later, Astrakhan. The Siberian Khanate gradually
disappeared as the Russian farmers moved east, and
ploughed up the pasture lands. The Mongols in the
Crimea held out until the reign of Catherine the
Great (1762–96), when they were conquered by
General Suvorov. However, by then, the Mongols
were no longer a threat to the security of Russia.

Mongols today

Today, about three million Mongols live on the lands where Genghis Khan and his followers once wandered. They are divided amongst the People's Republic of Outer Mongolia, the Buryat and Tiwa Autonomous Republics of the U.S.S.R., and the Chinese province of Inner Mongolia.

In the Russian provinces, most of the herds were collectivized during the 1930s, and the mineral wealth of the country was exploited. Most Mongols gave up their traditional way of life, and went to work in mines and factories. Those that still live in yurts have wooden floors, central heating and electric light. Most of them, however, live in Western-style houses or apartment blocks. Their customs and way of life have been deeply influenced by the spread of Communism, and the necessity of doing national service, which brought them into contact with people from totally different cultural backgrounds.

The Mongols of the People's Republic of Outer Mongolia have had to face constant pressure from both the Russians and the Chinese. So far they have managed to survive. Financial and technical aid has enabled them to start their own industries, but many of their people have kept to the old way of life. Dressed in dels, they wander with their herds over a land, mostly desert, seven times the size of Britain. They set up their yurts where they like, and sing about the heroes of the past.

The Mongols in China have suffered most of all. They have been separated from their own people, and their pasture lands have been ploughed up by Chinese immigrants. They have had either to adapt themselves to the new conditions or die out.

A few stubbornly refused to accept change, and tried to escape from bondage. In the early 1950s,

Opposite In the face of twentieth-century civilization, few of the Mongols retain their nomadic way of life. These hunters and trappers, however, still follow the fur-bearing animals whose skins are so valuable on the international market.

Below A member of the Udegeh tribe playing a traditional Mongol instrument.

some tribes fled from their homes in Turkestan and Sinkiang, and made their way across to Turkey. At the end of a long and bitter journey, only 2,000 out of the original 18,000 had survived.

So the Mongols have ceased to be the destroyers of civilization, and have become its victims. For generation after generation, they promised themselves that "when the Tsar of Russia and the Son of Heaven in China vanish, a new Genghis Khan will arise and recreate the worldwide Mongol Empire." These rulers are no more, but where is the new Mongol leader?

Principal Characters

ARIK-BUKA Tolui's youngest son. Tried to seize the throne but was defeated by his elder brother, Kublai. Died in 1264.

BATU Juchi's eldest son. The conqueror of Russia and founder of the Golden Horde. Died in 1256.

BERKE Juchi's younger son, and third Khan of the Golden Horde in Russia. Died in 1266.

BORTEI Timujin's principal wife and daughter of Dai-Sechen, chief of the Konkurats.

HOELUN Mother of Timujin.

HULAGU Third son of Tolui. Led the conquest of the Near East. Became the first Mongol ruler of Persia as Ilkhan. Died in 1265.

JAGATAI Genghis's second son. Became the first Khan of Turkestan.

JAMUGA Chief of the Juriats, and blood-brother of Timujin. Later became one of his principal opponents. Executed by Timujin.

JEBEI-NOYAN One of Genghis's greatest generals. Conquered the Kara-Khitai, and led the first expedition into Russia.

JELAL-UD-DIN Son of Shah Muhammad of Khwarizm. Fought bravely against Genghis before escaping to Persia.

JUCHI Genghis's eldest son. Uncertain parentage since Bortei had been carried off before his birth. Quarrelled with his brother Jagatai, and was demoted. Died in 1226.

KABUL Khan of the Mongols and Timujin's great-grandfather. Killed by the Kin Chinese in 1135.

KAIDAN Ogedai's son, who opposed Kublai's interest in China. Led a successful uprising in Central Mongolia.

KITBOGA Hulagu's second-in-command in the Near East. Was defeated at Ain Jalut (1260).

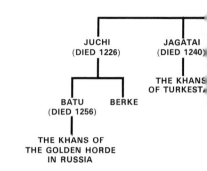

JUCHI (DIED 1226) — JAGATAI (DIED 1240)

THE KHANS OF TURKESTAN

BATU (DIED 1256) — BERKE

THE KHANS OF THE GOLDEN HORDE IN RUSSIA

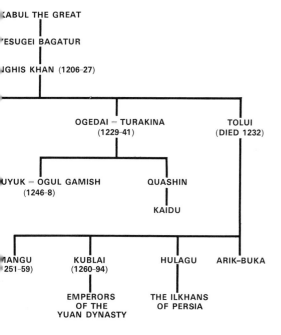

KABUL THE GREAT

YESUGEI BAGATUR

GHIS KHAN (1206–27)

OGEDAI = TURAKINA   TOLUI
(1229–41)   (DIED 1232)

UYUK = OGUL GAMISH   QUASHIN
(1246–8)

KAIDU

MANGU   KUBLAI   HULAGU   ARIK-BUKA
1251–59)   (1260–94)

EMPERORS   THE ILKHANS
OF THE   OF PERSIA
YUAN DYNASTY

KUBLAI   Third son of Tolui, and last of the Great Khans. Became Emperor of all China. Died in 1294.

KUCHLUK   Chief of the Naiman, and ruler of Kara-Khitai. One of Genghis's chief opponents. Defeated and killed by Jebei in 1217.

KUYUK   Son of Ogedai. Elected Khan in 1246. Died, probably poisoned, in 1248.

MANGU   Eldest son of Tolui. Elected Khan in 1251. Died on campaign in China in 1259.

MUHAMMAD   Shah of Khwarizm. Defeated by Genghis and died in 1221.

OGEDAI   Genghis's third son. Named by Genghis as his successor. Died while his armies were invading Europe in 1241.

OGUL-GAMISH   Kuyuk's principal wife, and regent between 1248 and 1251. Dabbled in black magic.

SUBODAI   One of the greatest Mongol generals. Organized the raids into Russia and Europe.

TAYAN   Chief of the Naiman. Tried but failed to unite the tribes against Timujin. Was killed in battle.

TIMUJIN   Son of Yesugei, great-grandson of Kabul. Became Genghis Khan, "Khan of Khans" in 1206. Reformed Mongol society, founded the Mongol empire, and earned the title "The World Conqueror." (1167–1227).

TOLUI   Genghis's youngest and best-loved son. Father of Mangu, Kublai, Hulagu and Arik-Buka.

TUGRAL   Chief of the Keraits. Adopted Timujin and at first helped him. Later became jealous and attacked him. Was killed by Timujin in 1203.

TURAKINA   Ogedai's principal wife and regent from 1242 to 1246. Engineered the election of her eldest son, Kuyuk, as Great Khan.

YESUGEI-BAGATUR   Timujin's father. Mongol chief of moderate ability. Poisoned by the Tartars in 1175.

Table of Dates

1242–46	Ogedai's widow Turakina acts as regent.
1246	The pope sends John of Plano Carpini to Karakorum. He witnesses Kuyuk's coronation.
1248	Death of Kuyuk.
1248–51	Khatum Ogul-Gamish, Kuyuk's widow, acts as regent, and dabbles in black magic.
1251	Mangu elected Khan.
1255	William of Rubruck offers Mangu an alliance with King Louis IX of France.
1256	Hulagu exterminates the Assassins in the mountains of Persia.
1258	Capture and destruction of Baghdad.
1259	Mangu dies in China. Hulagu draws back into Persia with his army, leaving Kitboga to continue the conquest of the Near East.
1260	Kitboga is defeated by the Egyptian Mamelukes at Ain-Jalut. Kublai elected Khan.
1267	Kublai sets out to win over Sung China.
1271	Kublai is recognized as Emperor of northern China.
1275	Marco Polo arrives at Kublai's court.
1276	Kublai becomes Emperor of the whole of China.
1286	The Manchus invade northern China. Kublai defeats them near the Liao River.
1291	Kublai sends an invasion fleet to Japan, which is destroyed by the "Kamikaze" wind.
1294	Death of Kublai Khan.
1368	The last Mongol Emperor is driven out of China. Foundation of the Ming dynasty.
1502	Break-up of the Golden Horde in Russia.
1911	The Chinese Revolution. Outer Mongolia declares itself independent.
1917	The Russian Revolution. Russian Mongolia becomes part of Soviet Russia.
1924	Autonomous Mongolian People's Republic set up in Outer Mongolia.

Glossary

ASSASSINS A group of Moslem fanatics who murdered all their opponents.

AUTOCRAT An absolute ruler.

AVENTAIL A hood or cowl of mail which the Mongols wore under their helmets to protect their neck and shoulders.

BAGATUR Literally "the brave." It came to mean the leader of a group of a hundred men in the Mongol army.

BALLISTA A giant crossbow or catapult used in siege warfare.

BRIDEPRICE Property or money given by a husband to his wife's father, to compensate him for the loss of his daughter's services.

BUDDHIST Someone who follows the teachings of the Indian religious leader, Gautama Buddha.

CALIPH A Moslem ruler, in charge of both civil and religious affairs.

CAPSTAN A machine for winding up ropes, which consisted of a revolving barrel turned by levers.

CENSORS Officials appointed by Kublai Khan in an attempt to stop corruption among civil servants.

CHARQUI Meat which the Mongols cut up into strips and dried in the sun.

CHRONICLER An early historian, who described what he saw happening around him.

COLLECTIVIZE To take land, property, etc., from private owners, and put it under the control of the state.

CRUSADER A Christian soldier who fought the Moslems in Palestine to regain possession of the Holy Land.

DEL A long coat, open all the way down the front and fastened across the chest.

HAUBERK A long coat of mail.

KHAN   The elected leader of a Mongol tribe; also used in general terms to mean a Mongol emperor.

KHARACHU   An ordinary soldier in the Mongol army, and owner of a small plot of land.

KOUMISS   A nourishing alcoholic drink made from mare's milk.

KNOUT   A three-stringed rawhide whip.

KURILTAI   A meeting of all the Mongol tribal leaders.

KURIYEN   A group of Mongol tents arranged in a circle.

LAMELLAR   Used to describe armour made out of thin strips of metal (*lamellae*) sewn onto a leather tunic.

MANGONEL   A siege engine for throwing stones or other missiles.

MOSLEM   A follower of the prophet Mohammed.

NOMAD   A tribesman who wanders with his herd in search of pasture.

NOYAN   Title given to the leader of a thousand men in the Mongol army.

SAMURAI   A professional Japanese soldier.

SHAMAN   A Mongol priest, magician, doctor and fortune-teller.

STEPPES   The vast, grass-covered plains of Central Asia.

TOTEM   An animal which is sacred to a particular group of people.

TREBUCHET   A giant sling used in siege warfare.

TRIBUTE   Money or goods paid regularly by one state to another as a token of submission.

TUNDRA   The marshy plains in the north of Siberia, which are covered with lichens and moss.

ULUS   A band of Mongol warriors serving a warlord.

WINDLASS   A machine for lifting weights, consisting of a crank handle and a drum, around which a rope is wound.

YASA   The code of laws set out by Genghis Khan.

YURT   A Mongol tent.

Further Reading

B. Bartos-Hoppner, *The Cossacks* (Oxford University Press, 1962) – tales from Cossack lands.

Hans Baumann, *Sons of the Steppe* (Oxford University Press, 1959) – the story of Genghis Khan, and of the ambitions of his sons and grandsons.

W. Fairservis, *Horsemen of the Steppes* (Brockhampton Press, 1963) – mainly about the steppes, but there is a good chapter on Genghis Khan himself.

Peter Fleming, *News from Tartary* (Jonathan Cape, 1936) – excellent background reading about life in the steppes.

N. Gogol, *Taras Bulba and Other Tales* (Dent, Everyman edition) – more tales from the steppes, by the great Russian story-teller.

H. Hookham, *Tamberlaine the Conqueror* (Hodder & Stoughton, 1962) – a history of his life and conquests.

Louise A. Kent, *He went with Marco Polo* (Harrap, 1936) – an "eye-witness" account of Marco Polo's journey into China.

Charles King, *The Story of Genghis Khan* (Dent, 1971) – his life and times.

T. Talbot Rice, *The Scythians* (Thames & Hudson, 1957) – a history of these fierce warriors.

Jules Verne, *Michael Strogoff* (Arco, 1964) – an adventure story in Jules Verne's best tradition.

F. Wurthle, *The Prince of Fergana* (Abelard-Schumann, 1962) – story set in the mountains and valleys of Central Asia.

Index

Picture Credits

The author and publishers wish to thank all those who have given
permission for the reproduction of copyright illustrations on the
following pages: Mansell collection, 10, 16–17, 26, 30 (top), 43, 47, 53
(top), 54–55, 62, 63, 70, 71, 74, 82–83; Mary Evans Picture Library,
25; Target Films International, 22–23; Novosti Press Agency, 45,
74–75, 85, 86, 87; Radio Times Hulton Picture Library, *frontispiece*,
9, 12, 14, 15, 16, 19, 27, 30 (bottom), 34–35, 38–39, 42, 53 (bottom),
59, 60–61, 65, 66, 72–73, 76, 77, 78–79, 80, 83; the Trustees of the
British Museum, *jacket* (front and flaps); the Trustees of the Victoria
& Albert Museum, *jacket* (back).
The maps and drawings were done by John Walters.